★ **PRIZE-WINNING** Science Fair Projects ★

BUILD YOUR OWN ROBOT
Science Fair Projects

Ed Sobey, Ph.D.

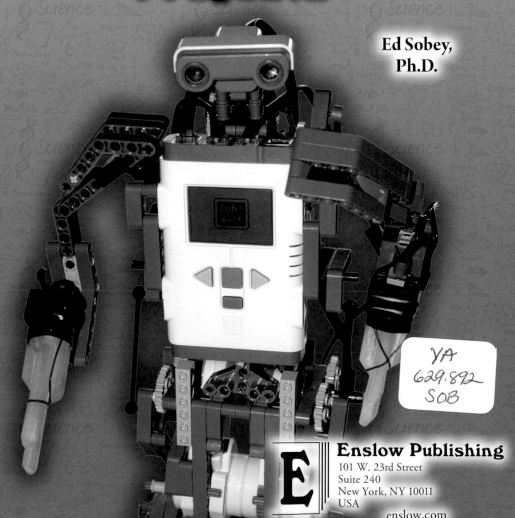

E **Enslow Publishing**
101 W. 23rd Street
Suite 240
New York, NY 10011
USA

enslow.com

To A. C. Gilbert, a man whose toys inspired generations of engineers, inventors, and scientists, including me

Published in 2016 by Enslow Publishing, LLC
101 W. 23rd Street, Suite 240, New York, NY 10011

Cataloging-in-Publication Data

Sobey, Ed.
  Build your own robot science fair project / by Ed Sobey, Ph.D.
      p. cm. — (Prize-winning science fair projects)
  Includes bibliographical references and index.
  ISBN 978-0-7660-7018-9 (library binding)
  1. Robotics — Juvenile literature. 2. Science projects — Juvenile literature. I. Sobey, Edwin J. C., 1948-. II. Title.
  TJ211.2 S63 2016
  629.8'92—d23

Printed in the United States of America

To Our Readers: We have done our best to make sure all Web site addresses in this book were active and appropriate when we went to press. However, the author and the publisher have no control over and assume no liability for the material available on those Web sites or on any Web sites they may link to. Any comments or suggestions can be sent by e-mail to customerservice@enslow.com.

Portions of this book originally appeared in the book *How to Build Your Own Prize-Winning Robot*.

Illustration Credits: Stephen F. Delisle with modification by Accurate Art, Inc. c/o George Barile.

Photo Credits: © Ed Sobey except bbbb/Shutterstock.com, p. 1 (robot); CHEN WS/Shutterstock.com, pp. 8, 33, 113; Martynova Anna/Shutterstock.com, p. 73; Maureen Sullivan/Moment Mobile/Getty Images, p. 67; NASA, p. 15; Ohn Mar/Shutterstock.com (science background throughout book); science photo/Shutterstock.com, p. 102; YASUYOSHI CHIBA/AFP/Getty Images, p. 11.

Cover Credits: bbbb/Shutterstock.com (robot); Ohn Mar/Shutterstock.com (science background).

CONTENTS

Acknowledgments 5

Introduction 7

CHAPTER 1 Learn About Robots 10

⭐ **PROJECT 1:** Building a Motorized Model Boat 18

⭐ **PROJECT 2:** Building a Motorized Model Car 28

CHAPTER 2 Learn About Electric Motors .. 38

PROJECT 3: Taking a Motor Apart 41

⭐ **PROJECT 4:** Measuring Voltages with a Voltmeter 44

PROJECT 5: Measuring Voltage Drops and Current 49

CHAPTER 3 How to Modify Servos 54

PROJECT 6: Hacking the Servos 56

CHAPTER 4 Add Some Wheels 61

PROJECT 7: Attaching the Motors to the Wheels 64

CHAPTER 5 Build a Robot Platform 67

⭐ **PROJECT 8:** Building the Platform 68

PROJECT 9: Attaching the Wheels and
Motors to the Platform.................. 72

PROJECT 10: Attaching the Circuit Board 75

CHAPTER 6 Supply Electrical Power 76

PROJECT 11: Series and Parallel Circuits 80

CHAPTER 7 Control the
Robot's Motion 82

PROJECT 12: Wire the Circuit Board 85

PROJECT 13: Running Servos with a Stamp Chip 89

Experiments with a ⭐ symbol feature Project Ideas and Further Explorations.

PROJECT 14: Moving the Robot in a Straight Line 94

PROJECT 15: Completing the Square 99

CHAPTER 8 What Else Can the Robot Do? 100

CHAPTER 9 Robot Competitions and Science Fair Projects 112

APPENDIX A: Robot Kits and Supplies 118

APPENDIX B: Other Approaches to Robotics 122

APPENDIX C: Robotics Clubs and Organizations 123

Further Reading 124

Web Sites 126

Index 127

Acknowledgments

Several robot professionals and avid hobbyists helped with technical details. Gene Elliott and other members of the Seattle Robotics Society provided references and background information.

Ken Gracey of Parallax contributed components I used to build model robots.

Texas BEST, Texas A&M University, and Texas Instruments invited me to their robot competition and inspired this book. Thank you, gracious hosts.

I am deeply indebted to Ted Mahler, cofounder of BEST and design engineer for Texas Instruments, for reviewing the manuscript and giving valuable suggestions.

Most of the photos were taken at robot camps and classes, especially Kids Invent Robots.

Introduction

Robots are a hot topic everywhere. Autonomous automobiles are now driving the streets and robotic helicopters are snapping photos from the sky. Some companies are developing parcel delivery services run by robots or robot-like devices. The greatest change in the field of robots is that the technology is now accessible and affordable. You can build robots, and this book will be your starting point.

Robotics involves electronics, mechanical systems, computers, and a variety of materials. This book will guide you through the most important elements of these fields. The starting point is getting you familiar and comfortable with electric motors and motor control.

Each chapter will give you information you need to build your robot, as well as specific examples and projects. Chapters 1 and 2 help you learn about robots, circuits, and motors. Beginning with Project 6 in Chapter 3, you can follow the projects from chapter to chapter using the suggested materials to make your own robot. You may, however, choose to create an original robot using different components from electronics, model, and robot stores. The Project Ideas and Further Exploration sections will give you ideas for different robot options.

As much as we hope you will enjoy reading about robots, we urge you to make one. Or make two. Learning is in the making, and you will learn so much while making your robot work the way you want it to.

At the 2012 World Robot Olympaid in Malaysia, these students watch their robots play soccer using programmed responses.

The Scientific Method

When you do a science project, especially one with your own original research, you will need to use what is commonly called the scientific method. In many textbooks you will find a section devoted to the subject. The scientific method consists of a series of steps.

1. Come up with a **QUESTION** or try to solve a **PROBLEM**. What are you curious about? What could your robot do?
2. **RESEARCH** your topic. Find out what is already known. Has anyone already answered your question or solved your problem? What facts are published about your topic?
3. Form a **HYPOTHESIS**, which is an answer to your question or a solution to your problem.
4. Design an **EXPERIMENT** to test your hypothesis. Collect and record the data from your experiment.
5. Study your experimental **RESULTS** and form a **CONCLUSION**. Was your hypothesis true or false?
6. **REPORT** your findings.

Safety First

Always follow these safety rules while working on your robots.

- Do not use electric current from a wall or floor outlet except for devices that have been tested and approved.
- Do not point sharp tools toward yourself or others.
- Protect your eyes with glasses or safety goggles.
- Get adult help before using any power tools or gasoline motors.

This book will launch you into designing and building your own robots. Have fun and be safe.

Chapter 1

LEARN ABOUT ROBOTS

Robots have invaded Hollywood. WALL-E, Chappie, and Johnny 5 joined R2-D2 and C-3PO from the *Star Wars* movies as modern heroes. But you can't rush out to buy one of these marvelous machines, you will have to make one.

Real robots are unlike the ones you see in the movies. Most of the movie robots aren't robots at all. What makes a machine a robot?

To be a robot, a machine has to meet three criteria. First, it has to do mechanical work. That is, it must be able to move itself or move something else. So a computer is not a robot. In a factory, robots most often retrieve parts and put them where they are needed to assemble something. Sometimes they weld parts together. Other robots operate spray painters. Whatever else it does, a robot moves.

Second, robots can perform a variety of tasks. A machine that can only do one job is not a robot. The versatility of robots makes them special among machines.

Third, robots are controlled by a set of computer instructions that can be reprogrammed. By changing the computer program, you can change what a robot does. For example, you could program

A robot arm carries a car to the next step in the assembly line in a factory. There are three things that make a robot: it moves, it can perform different tasks, and it is controllable and reprogrammable.

a robot to move forward until it detects a light and then move toward the light. Many robots store such instructions in an onboard memory device. Others have onboard computers that do nothing but control the robot.

Apply these criteria to a typical device, the lawn mower. If the lawn mower is self-propelled it meets the first criteria of moving. However, it cannot pass the second criteria, because to use its engine for something else, like powering a go-cart, you would have to take the lawn mower apart. It also fails the third criteria, because you cannot program it. You must push it or walk behind it to steer it.

For robots to be useful they need to be able to collect and process information about their surroundings. Picture a robot cutting your lawn. Without guidance it could drive into the neighbor's yard. Each time one of its drive wheels slipped a fraction of an inch, the robot would go off course. Since all mechanical systems slip and get misaligned, robots have to have sensors that let them realign themselves.

The robot would need to determine when it was at the end of the yard and which way it should turn to go back. It might need to be able to determine the height of the grass to decide if certain sections needed to be cut. It would need a separate sensor to stop cutting grass when the catch bag was full.

Robots also need sensors for safety. The robot mowing your lawn would need to stop before it ran into a person, pet, or tree. An optical sensor could warn it if something was five feet in front of it so it could shut off the engine.

To process the information gathered from their sensors, robots use computers. Computers interpret these signals, make decisions about them, and generate responses. In the example of a robot that cuts lawns, an operator could reprogram the robot to cut grass at different heights, depending on how the grass was growing. The robot would make a decision by comparing the height of grass in front of it to the desired height input by the operator. It could also sense rainfall and decide, based on its programmed instructions, to quit cutting and head for the shed.

To understand robots, it is helpful to compare them to humans. Where robots have sensors (usually electronic, but also physical-contact), humans have senses (touch, hearing, smell, sight, and taste); where robots have computers, humans have brains. Robots, however, can respond only in ways humans have programmed them. They cannot respond creatively or spontaneously.

Robots are not human. They are machines that combine the information-gathering, storing, and processing capabilities of computers with a variety of machines that can move and do work.

People often confuse remote controlled machines with robots. By the strict definition of robots, remote controlled devices do not qualify. To be a true autonomous, or self-governing robot, a machine must be capable of working on its own once it has been programmed. Machines operated by humans with either wire or radio controls are not robots.

When people think of robots, most think of the mobile ones they see in movies. Chappie walks and WALL-E and Johnny 5 roll. It is difficult to build a walking robot, which has to shift its weight with each step. ASIMO is one robot, but it costs millions. It is easier to build rolling robots. The easiest-to-build rolling robots steer them-selves not by turning a set of wheels like a car does, but by running two motors (each attached to one wheel or track) at different speeds and directions. This is the best model to start with. The experience of building this model can help you try more complex designs.

Robots are not confined to walking or rolling. People build airplane robots, boat robots, and submarine robots, too. However, most robots are not mobile.

Most industrial robots are fixed in place and move materials or hold and use tools. The robotic arms on space shuttles move satellites out of the storage bays for launching. Although this book will provide some suggestions on building robotic arms, it will focus on mobile robots.

A Short History of Robots

The word *robot* was coined not by an industrial engineer, but by a Czechoslovakian playwright, Karel Capek. He introduced the "robota," meaning drudgery or compulsory work, in a play in 1921. In his play, a man created a robot to do his work, but the robot ended up killing the man. Capek's imagination was far ahead of technology, as computers were rudimentary then and unable to control machines.

Before Capek imagined machines that could move by themselves, people operated machines. Until 1801, machines were dumb in the sense that people had to guide them each step of the way. Then Joseph Jacquard invented a programmable loom in France. He used cards with holes as maps for looms to follow for weaving patterns in cloth. His cards were the forerunners of computer punch cards. Many punch cards were fed into a machine, and depending on the location of the holes on the cards, the machine did certain things.

American inventor Herman Hollerith made the step from using cards in weaving patterns to using them in data processing. He applied Jacquard's idea to tabulating and sorting information for the U.S. census in the 1880s. He sold his company and it became part

A robotic arm on the International Space Station moves objects into and out of its docking port. Here, it is grabbing a cargo space-craft.

of IBM. His punch-card system, much improved, was used until the advent of personal computers nearly a century later.

George Devol designed the first programmable robot in 1954 and later started the first company to manufacture robots. General Motors purchased the first industrial robot, which picked up and moved parts. After seeing the value of the robot, General Motors ordered sixty-six more to weld parts on its assembly lines.

Researchers at Stanford University developed the first robot arm in 1970. In 1976, space probes *Viking 1* and *Viking 2* used a later version of this arm controlled by a microcomputer.

In the early 1980s, the South Florida Science Museum in West Palm Beach, Florida, built the first robot to give guided tours. "Sir Plus" was made of surplus parts. It followed a path of conducting foil taped to the floor and stopped at prearranged points to give visitors information about the exhibits. Wax or dirt on the floor sometimes interfered with the conducting foil and Sir Plus would wander aimlessly about the museum until it crashed into something or someone. The South Florida Science Museum retired it after a few years of service.

Although Japanese companies were years behind U.S. companies in their ability to use and make industrial robots, they quickly caught up. Today, Japan is the leading manufacturer and user of robots.

Tool List

Having the right tools makes the job easier. The following is a list of the tools you will need when you are making your robot. Each project in this book lists the specific materials you will need for that project. If you do not have or cannot get all of the items listed here, get started anyway, and be creative in figuring out how you can complete your robot without them.

- Screwdrivers—a variety of sizes for slotted and Phillips screws
- Jeweler's screwdrivers (smaller screwdrivers)
- Wire cutters
- Diagonal cutters
- Pliers—needle-nose and regular
- Wire stripper
- Coping saw
- Hot glue gun and glue sticks
- Scissors
- Measuring tape
- Square
- Safety goggles
- Hammers—claw and mallet
- Files and rasps
- Drill and bits
- Multimeter (voltmeter)
- Workbench with vice
- PC computer with CD-ROM drive
- Awl or sharp nail

BUILDING A MOTORIZED MODEL BOAT

This project introduces electric motors and circuits. Although the finished model is a motorized boat and not a robot, building it is a good way to become familiar with motors and circuits.

To make a boat hull, cut a quart or half-gallon milk carton in half lengthwise. (See Figure 1.) This gives two flat-bottomed hulls. Set the hulls aside.

You need to make an electric circuit to run the motor. A circuit is the path that electrical current will take. For this project, you want to power the boat's electric motor with a battery, so the circuit will be the path from one side of the battery to one of the terminals on the electric motor, to the other motor terminal, and then back to the other side of the battery. If this circuit is

Materials:

* quart or half-gallon cardboard milk container
* propeller from a toy or model store, or made from aluminum foil
* small electric motors from an electronics or hobby store
* wire (22-gauge) or alligator clip leads
* D-cell battery
* $\frac{1}{4}$-inch dowel and pencil sharpener or sandpaper
* duct tape
* masking tape
* clear tape
* scissors
* wire cutters
* drill and bits
* awl or sharp nail
* hot glue gun and glue sticks
* bathtub or pool of water

complete, or closed, electricity will flow through it, spinning the motor. (See Figure 2.)

With wire cutters, cut some wire into two 20-cm (8-in) pieces. Strip about half an inch of the insulation off both ends of each piece. Attach one end of each wire to the electric motor. If the motor has wire leads, twist the exposed end of one wire onto one of the leads; connect the other piece of

A direct current (DC) motor

wire to the other lead the same way. If the motor does not have wire leads, wrap the exposed wire around the motor terminals, which are flat pieces of metal protruding from the motor. Tape the wires in place with masking tape.

Touch the loose ends of each piece of wire to the two terminals on the D-cell battery. You should hear a high-pitched whine as the electric motor spins.

You will be mounting the battery and motor in the hull and connecting a propeller to the motor. Secure the battery to the inside of one of the milk carton halves (hull) with a piece of duct tape, leaving the terminals free so you can connect them to the wires.

In a bathtub or large sink, check how low the hull floats with the battery and motor onboard. Mark the carton where the surface of the water meets the back of the boat. This is the waterline.

You will want the propeller to be just below the waterline, so you may need to angle the propeller shaft downward. You can get the angle you need by propping up the motor on a wedge cut from the other half of the milk carton.

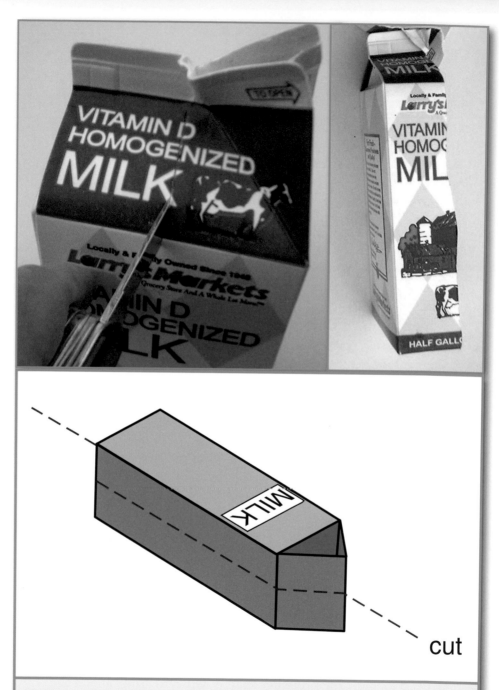

Figure 1. Cut a milk carton in half. Use one half to create the boat hull for your motorized model boat.

To make the propeller shaft, cut a 15-cm (6-in) length of ¼-inch dowel. Sharpen one end in a pencil sharpener or sand it to a point. You will be sliding the propeller onto the sharpened end. **Ask an adult** to drill a small hole in the center of the other end of the dowel so the motor shaft will fit into it.

If you don't have a propeller, you can make one. Cut a piece of aluminum foil 5 cm × 2 cm (2 in × 1 in). Fold it in half lengthwise, and then widthwise. Twist the ends in opposite directions. (See Figure 3.) Use an awl or nail to poke a small hole in the center of the propeller. (To find the center, balance it on the awl.) **Make sure you are pointing the sharp end away from you and others.** Jam the pointed end of the ¼-inch dowel into the hole in the propeller and hot glue it in place.

To make the hole in the center of the back of the boat at the waterline, poke a hole through the hull with the awl or nail. Slide the propeller shaft through the hole to the motor shaft.

You will now secure the motor to the hull of the boat. Use a small piece of the milk carton to prop up the motor so the propeller shaft angles downward, keeping the propeller in the water. When you have adjusted the motor to the right angle, hot glue it to the piece of the milk carton and hot glue this motor stand to the hull. Be careful not to get glue inside the motor. (See Figure 4.)

Take your boat to a bathtub, swimming pool, or small pond to test it. Use a piece of duct tape to hold the wires to the battery terminals. If the motor does not run, press the wires to the battery to ensure that they are making contact. Put the boat in the water and prepare to be splashed. **Never use your boat in a pool or pond without an adult present.**

If the boat steers to one side, try repositioning the motor. For example, if it steers to the left, move the motor one centimeter

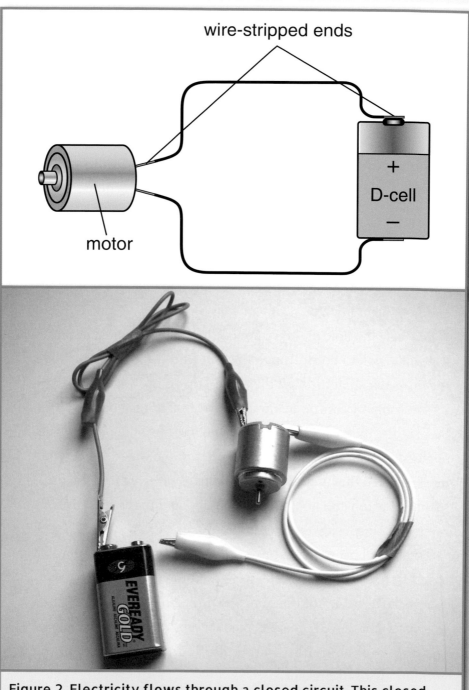

wire-stripped ends

+
D-cell
−

motor

Figure 2. Electricity flows through a closed circuit. This closed circuit has wire connecting the battery and the motor.

Figure 3. An aluminum foil propeller is glued to the shaft that connects to the DC motor.

(half an inch) to the left. This will angle the propeller to the right, which will push the bow to the right. You can also add a keel to the bottom of the boat to help it travel in a straight line. A keel is the long projection along the center of the bottom of a boat. Make the keel out of a 5 cm × 12.5 cm (2 in × 5 in) rectangle cut from a milk carton. Duct tape the short side onto the bottom of the boat so it is aligned fore and aft (the same distance from the front and back) and projecting down into the water.

If the boat goes backward instead of forward, one solution is to switch the wires connected to the battery. The wire that had been connected to the positive end should now connect to the negative end and vice versa. (Look for the symbols "+" and "–" to tell you which end of the battery is positive and which is negative.) This switches the flow of electricity through the motor, which reverses the direction of its spin and thus the direction of the propeller's spin.

Another way to reverse the boat's direction is to reshape the propeller. If you made the propeller out of aluminum foil, twist the ends in opposite directions.

How can you get the motor to spin slower or faster? To get it spinning faster, you can increase the voltage in the circuit by adding a second battery. Try this by taping the positive (+) end of one battery to the negative (–) end of a second battery. Connect the wires to the outside contacts of the two-battery power cell.

To get the motor spinning slower, you must reduce the voltage. If you have a small electric light, you can add it to the circuit; some of the battery's energy will be expended lighting the light, which will reduce the energy available to the motor. The light adds electrical "resistance" to the circuit and reduces the current in the circuit. To do this, remove one wire from the battery and connect it to one

Short Circuit Danger!

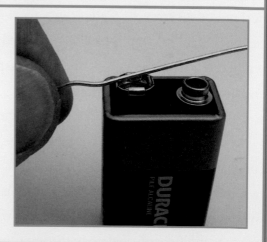

If you connect the two battery terminals directly with a piece of wire, you will make a "short circuit." A short circuit will quickly ruin the battery and could burn you, so make sure you avoid short circuits.

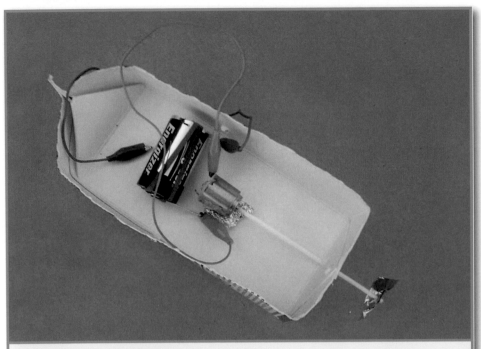

Figure 4. The finished electric boat model is ready to test in a bathtub or wading pool.

terminal of the light. Use another piece of wire to connect the other side of the light to the battery.

PROJECT IDEA AND FURTHER EXPLORATION

By adding a second motor and propeller you can control the boat's motion better. If you have a second motor and propeller available, make a two-motor boat. You will need the boat model you made in Project 1, a second battery, a second propeller, a second motor, and additional wire.

Remove the first motor, shaft, and propeller. Tape (duct) over the hole you made in the hull for the propeller shaft. Make two new holes along the back of the boat, about 1 inch from each corner.

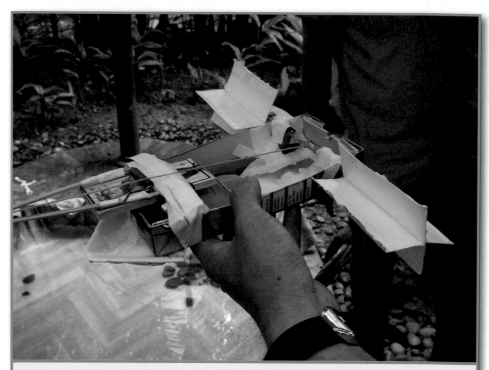

If you liked building the electric boat, try this model. Instead of having a propeller, this model uses two paddles cut from another milk carton. They are powered by the same motor, but the power is delivered to a shaft holding the two paddles by a rubber band.

Install into the new holes the two motors, shafts, and propellers as you did before.

Having two motors gives you much better directional control. Try running one motor forward and the other backward to turn the boat. If you made the propellers out of aluminum foil, see what happens if you twist them in opposite directions (twist one clockwise and the other counterclockwise). With the propellers having opposite "pitches," or twists, run one motor in reverse. Does that give better control?

BUILDING A MOTORIZED MODEL CAR

The electric car you make in this project will have the same electric circuit as did the boat in Project 1. The major difference between the two projects is how you connect the motor to the drivetrain.

Cut a piece of sturdy cardboard 10 cm × 15 cm (4 in × 6 in) for the car body. Glue two 10-cm– (4-in–) long pieces of straw on one side of the cardboard body. Make sure the two straws are parallel to each other and are located near the edges of the cardboard.

You can purchase wheels at a hobby or craft store or you can take them from an old toy. Other wheel sources are DVDs, lids from gallon milk jugs, and other round lids. The challenge is to find the exact center (where the wheel balances) and to attach the wheel securely to the axle so it does not wobble.

Use wire cutters to cut the dowel into two pieces, each about 12 cm (5 in) long. If the dowel fits into the center opening of the wheel, place one wheel on each of the two dowels. (See Figure 5

Materials

* safety goggles or glasses
* 9V battery
* electric hobby motor
* wire (22-gauge) or alligator clip leads
* cardboard
* scissors
* 1/8-inch dowel
* 4 plastic wheels with 1/8-in center holes (from a craft store)
* plastic propeller that fits onto the motor shaft
* straws
* hot glue gun and glue sticks
* wire cutters

Figure 5. a) Push the wheel onto the end of a dowel. Insert the dowel into a straw that you can glue to the bottom of a piece of cardboard. b) The basic car model will roll easily across a table or smooth floor. The next step is to add a motor.

a.) Insert the other end of the dowels through the straws and then force the other wheels onto the dowels. The dowel pieces are now axles and the straw pieces are bearings that hold the axles in place while allowing them to turn. (See Figure 5b.)

If the wheels don't attach easily to the dowels, you will have to glue them. You could cut a small square of cardboard, poke a hole through it so you can insert the end of a dowel snugly. Glue the dowel into the cardboard and glue the cardboard square onto whatever you will use for a wheel. The difficult step in this operation is getting the dowel aligned in the center of the wheel. It needs to be very close for the car to roll easily.

When you have all four wheels attached to axles supported by the bearings, test the car. Do the wheels run along the side of the cardboard? Does the model roll easily on a smooth floor? The model should roll with just a slight push otherwise the motor will not be able to push it.

Push the propeller onto the motor shaft. It should fit snugly. (See Figure 6.) The forces on the propeller are strong enough to send it flying if it is not pushed firmly onto the motor shaft. When testing the motor and propeller, wear safety goggles or glasses just in case the propeller flies off.

Check to see how high the motor has to be so that the propeller does not hit the ground. Depending on the size of the wheels and the length of the propeller blades, you will have to raise the motor so the propeller clears the floor. Cut a small piece of cardboard (10 cm × 2.5 cm, or 4 in × 1 in) and fold it into a square. Glue the square to the car body so the motor can sit on top.

Hot glue an electric hobby motor to the cardboard square you just made, making sure the propeller will not hit either the car body or ground. Use a small dab of hot glue to secure the 9V battery to the body. You can later rip the motor and battery away from the cardboard if you use just a modest amount of glue.

The motor and battery are the only heavy components of this model so their weight should be balanced. If both are glued near one end of the model, it will likely flip over.

Connect one battery terminal to one motor terminal with an alligator clip lead or 22-gauge wire. Alligator clip leads are wires with springed jaws at each end that let you make temporary

Figure 6. Force the propeller onto the motor shaft. Have an adult help because it is essential that the propeller be pushed all the way onto the shaft.

Electric Motors

Inexpensive hobby motors run at high speeds. The typical speeds range between 10,000 and 17,000 RPM, or revolutions per minute. At 17,000 RPM, the surface of a 2.5-cm (1-in) wheel would move at about 50 miles per hour. (A 2.5-cm, or 1-in, wheel has a circumference of 3.14 inches and travels 17,000 times 3.14 inches per minute, or about 50 miles per hour.)

Although it might sound like fun to have a model car travel at that speed, it is too fast to control. Later, when you are building a robot, you will use motors that run at much lower, controllable speeds. Inexpensive hobby motors are not suitable for robots.

connections quickly. Before you connect the second clip lead, put your safety goggles or glasses on.

You are ready to test your car. Complete the circuit by attaching a second alligator clip lead or wire to the other battery terminal and the other motor terminal.

With a 9V battery the motor will spin the propeller very fast. You will hear the high-pitched hum and you will feel the breeze generated by the propeller. Release the car on a smooth floor and watch what happens.

Problems You May Encounter

If the motor does not spin when you connect it to the battery, check the electrical connections. Sometime you will find a clip lead that is defective.

If the motor spins but the car doesn't move, roll both front and rear wheels to make sure they can turn easily. Is the propeller pushing air in the opposite direction you want the model to move?

A young girl sits in a wheelchair robot during the 2012 World Robot Olympaid. The theme of the event was robots working with people.

9V batteries are an easy way to power models. But they run out of energy quickly and are very expensive for the power they provide. For most projects we will recommend using AA batteries held in a battery case.

If it is pushing air to one side or up or down, it is wasting energy that could be pushing the model forward.

Set up a short race course on the floor by marking a start and finish line. Use a smartphone app to time the model's race time and record this time. Then think of ways to make the car go faster. Try each idea one at a time and retest the car on the race course. Record the times and make notes on what you did to make the car go faster.

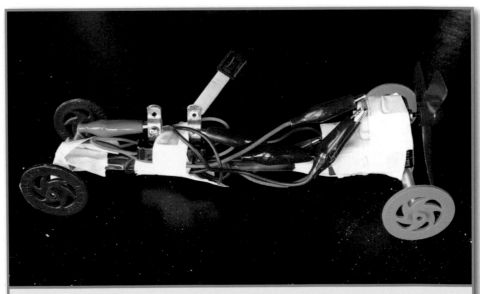

This model car has electric propeller drive. A knife blade switch has been added to the circuit to make it easier to turn the motor on and off.

Switch the wire that is on the positive (+) terminal of the battery to the negative (–) terminal, and the wire that is on the negative terminal to the positive. What happens to your car's motion?

The car you just made is a propeller-powered model. There are other ways to use the same motor to drive the car. You could attach a wheel directly to the motor shaft. To make it fit, wrap two turns of masking tape to the motor shaft and force it into the center opening of a wheel. If the wheel slips on a smooth floor, wrap it with a small section cut from the neck of a rubber balloon. (See Figure 7.)

Figure 7. If the wheel slides on a smooth floor, add a rubber tire. This one is made from the neck of a rubber balloon.

You could also try using a rubber band to connect one axle to the motor, much like a chain connects the rear wheel of a bike to the pedals. You will have to modify the car so you can get a rubber band onto an axle. You will also need to make sure the rubber band does not rub on the car body.

Other Types of Wheel Drivers

If you like to build car models, try making a direct drive car. Mount one wheel onto the motor shaft. You might have to wrap some masking tape around the shaft to get a tight fit.

Here's another model to try. Use a rubber band to drive one of the wheels or the axle at one end of the car. Angle the motor shaft away from the axle so the rubber band does not slide off the shaft.

Chapter 2

LEARN ABOUT ELECTRIC MOTORS

To appreciate how important electric motors are, walk through your home and count the number of electric motors you find. If you have a garage, check there, too. Many of the appliances in the kitchen have motors, as do clocks, electric pencil sharpeners, computer hard drives and disk drives, and power tools. Counting disk drives and hard drives, but not counting electric motors in cars, the author found thirty-five in his home.

A good place to start designing robots is by selecting the motors and wheels. This chapter covers motors, and the next chapter deals with wheels.

The motors have to be powerful enough to move the robot you are going to build. They also must afford you the ability to control them. You could not control the speed of the motors you used to make the car and boat in Chapter 1. They went on when you connected them to the battery and off when you disconnected them. They are fine for racing a car across the floor, but not for the precise moves a robot makes.

Motors convert electrical energy into mechanical energy, or motion. Inside the motor, electric current passes through loops of wire

Here are four types of direct current (battery-powered) motors (from left to right): stepper motor, servo motor, gear head motor, and toy motor.

to create an electromagnet. The north pole of this electromagnet is attracted to the south pole of a fixed magnet, which is also inside the motor. The fixed magnet is made of magnetized metal. (Touch a piece of steel or iron to the outside of the motor and notice the magnetic attraction.)

The electromagnet inside the motor spins on the motor shaft, so you would expect it to spin so its north pole is closest to the south pole of the fixed magnet. At that point, the spinning would stop. This would not be a useful motor.

To keep the motor spinning, the electromagnet changes its polarity just as it aligns its north pole with the fixed magnet's south pole.

What was the north pole of the electromagnet becomes the south pole. Magnetic forces push it away from the fixed magnet's south pole and toward the fixed magnet's north pole. When it gets there, its polarity will change again.

A big part of making an electric motor is making the electromagnet change its polarity as it spins. Changing the polarity requires that the electromagnet switch its connection with the battery from the positive terminal to the negative terminal and back again.

Taking a Motor Apart

Find a broken electrical appliance with a motor. Good devices to look for include electric typewriters, printers, DVD players, and disk drives. If you do not have any, check with friends, or look around at thrift stores or garage sales. People may be happy to give you an outdated or broken appliance. If taking apart appliances is new to you, get guidance from the author's book, *Unscrewed: Salvage and Reuse Motors, Gears, Switches, and More From Your Old Electronics.*

Materials

* old appliances, such as DVD players, electric typewriters, or battery-powered clocks
* screwdrivers
* wire cutters
* jeweler's screwdrivers
* pliers

Before you start to take an appliance apart, get permission from the owner. Cut off the electric cord with wire cutters. With pliers, bend the electrical prongs outward so no one can plug it into an outlet by mistake. Discard the wire and plug where children will not find it.

As you take the appliance apart, search for the motor. It will have electrical wires connected to it, and the motor shaft will connect to something that spins. Remove the motor and carefully take off its covering. Inside you will find permanent magnets (see if a screwdriver is attracted by them) and wire loops. See if you can figure out how it works.

Electric motors come in a wide variety of sizes and types. For your robot, you will want a motor that runs on direct current.

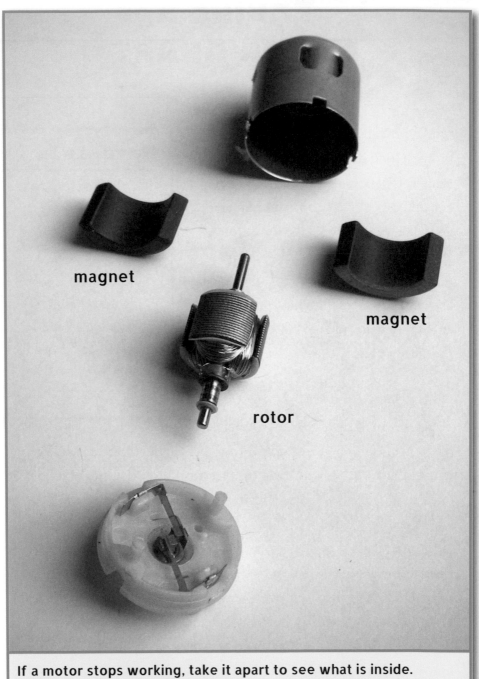

magnet

magnet

rotor

If a motor stops working, take it apart to see what is inside.
Here is a toy motor taken apart. You can see the two permanent
magnets and the rotor that spins between them.

Electric Motor History

Electric motors are one of the world's greatest inventions. British scientist Michael Faraday discovered the electromagnetic effect that makes motors spin. He first presented his results in 1821. In the United States, Thomas Davenport patented his motor in 1837 and made the first electric model train. Nikola Tesla invented the first electric motor to run on alternating current in 1888.

Direct current (DC) means that the electricity moves in one direction throughout the circuit, from one terminal of the battery, through the circuit, and back to the battery through the other terminal. Batteries supply direct current.

The electrical power from wall outlets is alternating current (AC). The voltage is not steady; it starts at zero volts, climbs to its maximum, drops back to zero, and reverses direction before going back to zero again. This cycle is like a wave on the ocean. However, it is repeated 60 times a second in the United States. It is described as 60 cycles per second, or 60 hertz (named to commemorate German physicist Heinrich Hertz). AC is much more powerful and dangerous than DC. It is difficult to transport in a moving robot and would require extension cords lying on the floor and getting in the path of the robots. You will use DC current exclusively to power your robot.

MEASURING VOLTAGES WITH A VOLTMETER

You can use a voltmeter to measure the voltage in the electric circuits you build. Inexpensive voltmeters cost about five dollars at an electronics store or from a catalog or Web-based retailer. It is one of the most useful tools for working with robots and electric projects. If you do not have one, ask the physical science teacher at your school if you can borrow one or use one at school.

Materials

* voltmeter or multimeter
* D-cell battery
* car or boat model from Projects 1 or 2
* alligator clip leads

Measure the voltage of a D-cell battery. Make sure the meter is set to measure DC volts, or DCV, direct current volts. Touch the voltmeter's positive lead wire to the positive terminal of the battery and touch the negative lead wire to the negative terminal of the battery. Does the reading match the voltage printed on the battery?

Connect the battery to the electric motor in one of the models you built and measure the voltage again. Holding all the wires plus the model and the voltmeter will require an extra pair of hands or a set of alligator clip leads. When the motor is running, the voltage will drop. With the motor still running, touch one finger to the motor shaft to slow it down and watch the voltmeter. (Don't let the plastic propeller hit your fingers. It will hurt!) As the workload increases (the motor is pushing against your finger), the voltage of the battery drops.

A fresh battery that is sized correctly (strong enough) for the motor will not experience a large voltage drop when connected to the motor. A battery that is almost dead will show a big drop in voltage with a load, even though it shows the rated voltage (printed on the battery's side) without a load.

PROJECT IDEA
AND FURTHER EXPLORATION

Try another experiment. Connect the voltmeter directly to the motor, and set the meter to its lowest direct current voltage scale. To do this on most meters, you rotate a large dial in the center. Spin the motor shaft between your fingers and watch the meter.

By spinning the shaft you are generating electricity. DC motors transform electricity into mechanical work (spinning) and can also transform mechanical work into electricity. Electrical power is generated this way. Water falls through giant turbines in dams, wind spins turbines in windmills, and steam spins turbines in power plants. To generate steam power, companies burn coal, natural gas, oil, or garbage, or they use nuclear reactors.

Three Kinds of Motors

To build a robot, you are going to use DC motors. The motors will run on low voltages (12 volts or less), so they can be powered with dry-cell batteries. The dry chemicals inside, actually a paste of chemicals, undergo a chemical reaction that converts chemical energy into electricity. Wet-cell batteries, the type used in cars, have liquid inside that lets electrons flow from one type of metal to another, generating electric currents.

There are three principal kinds of motors that use direct current: DC motors, stepper motors, and servos. In making the boat and car models, you used a DC motor. You can distinguish DC motors from the other two types by the number of wires or terminals. DC motors have two wires. Servos have three wires, and stepper motors can have as many as five or six.

As simple as DC motors are, they have limitations. They operate at high speeds. The shaft speed needed for a mobile robot is 75 to 150 RPMs, not the 17,000 RPMs typical for a hobby motor. Robotic arms require even slower motor speeds, typically 10 to 20 RPM.

One way to reduce the speed is to apply a lower voltage to the motor. You probably have experienced a motor slowing down as its battery weakens. At lower voltages however, the motors do not work effectively. Further, to be able to change voltage, and thus motor speed, requires wasting electrical energy by adding a variable resistor to the circuit. Part of the voltage from the battery will be expended heating up the resistor, and the remainder will spin the motor. Since battery power is limited in robots, we do not want to waste any. Although adding a variable resistor is an easy way to lower the available voltage and the speed of a DC motor, it is not an attractive option.

Speed in DC Motors

The problem of speed in DC motors can be handled by using slower motors and reduction gears. In a motor with reduction gears, the motor shaft spins a small gear with few teeth that meshes with a large gear that has many more teeth. Each revolution of the motor and the small gear partially rotates the large gear. If the small gear has 12 teeth and the large gear has 24, the large gear will turn half a revolution for every complete revolution of the small gear and motor shaft. Thus the large gear rotates at half the speed of the motor. If the large gear is attached to another small gear and

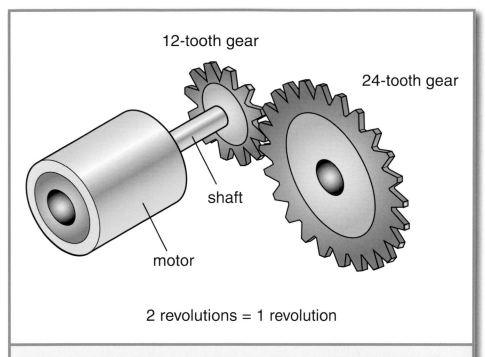

12-tooth gear

24-tooth gear

shaft

motor

2 revolutions = 1 revolution

Figure 8. Gears help to control the output of a motor. A 12-tooth gear is attached to a 24-tooth gear. Two revolutions of the smaller gear cause only one revolution of the larger gear.

the small gear meshes with another large gear, the output is cut in half again. (See Figure 8.) The combined reduction gear (two small gears meshing with two large gears) slows the speed of rotation to one quarter of the motor speed. To see gears in action, look inside mechanical toys, such as remote control cars, wind-up toys, and Push N' Go cars. Make sure you have the owner's permission to take apart the toy.

Stepper Motors

Stepper motors are an alternative to DC motors. While DC motors continue turning as long as electrical power is applied, stepper motors turn a fraction of a revolution and stop. To get a stepper motor to turn one complete revolution requires a series of electrical pulses (on and off). Printers and scanners use stepper motors to move the print head or scan device in tiny steps across a page. At each stop either ink is applied to the page or a scan reading is made, then the stepper motor moves to the next stop.

Stepper motors allow for precise motion. Many people use them in robots, but we will focus on the third alternative: servo motors, or servos.

Servo Motors

The third type of motor is a servo motor. Servos have a motor, reduction gears, a circuit board, and a position feedback device packaged in a rectangular plastic box. A circuit board is a plastic board that holds electronic components. A position feedback device measures how far a motor shaft has moved. This lets you program a motor to move a specific number of rotations of the shaft. When the motor has rotated far enough, the feedback device indicates this. Then the circuit board interrupts the flow of electricity to the motor.

You can identify servos by their three electrical wires. Two wires (black and red) supply electrical power, and the third wire (white) controls the motion. To control the speed and direction of the motor, a motor controller sends an electrical pulse 50 times a second through the third wire. Servos move through a limited range of motion and shut themselves off when they reach the end of that range. Thus, they are ideal for raising and lowering a car antenna or windows. Servos make good motors for robots because they turn slowly, are readily available, and are inexpensive. Also, they are easy to control with computers. We will discuss how to control motors in Chapter 7.

MEASURING VOLTAGE DROPS AND CURRENT

Voltages and currents are measured differently. In this project you will measure both the current running through a circuit and the voltage drop across a motor.

Pull out the two electric motors you used to make the boat in Project 1. Using alligator clip leads, connect one motor to a battery case holding 4 AA batteries. Note that each AA battery is rated at 1.5 volts; four of them connected in series will yield 6 volts.

Listen to the hum of the motor. Can you detect a difference in the pitch of the sound from the sound of the motor powered by the 9V battery?

Set the voltmeter to DCV for direct current volts. To measure the voltage drop across the battery, touch the positive (+) meter probe to the positive terminal of the battery case. The positive (+) and negative (−) symbols are shown on the side of the battery or are stamped beside the terminals. Connect the negative voltmeter lead to the negative battery case terminal and read the meter. The reading should be about 6 volts. In new batteries, the reading might be higher.

MATERIALS

* 8 AA batteries
* 2 battery cases that hold 4 AA batteries
* masking tape
* alligator clip leads
* voltmeter
* small electric motor
* newspaper
* aluminum foil

Voltmeters and multimeters allow you to test the voltage and current in a circuit. This meter is measuring the voltage in a 9V transistor battery.

Now disconnect the lead from the negative side of the battery. Change the voltmeter to measure DCA, or direct current amperes. Make sure it is set on the highest scale (set to measure the largest current). Connect the clip to the positive probe on the meter and use another clip lead to connect the negative probe to the negative side of the battery. Read and record the current. You may have to change scales on the meter to get a reading.

While voltage is measured in volts, current is measured in amperes. One ampere (or amp) is equal to the flow of 6.25×10^{18} electrons per second. A lighted 100-watt lightbulb has about 1 ampere of current flowing through it.

What would happen if you connected two motors in this circuit? Take the voltmeter out of the circuit. Connect one terminal of the second motor to the available terminal on the first motor. Connect the second terminal of the second motor to the battery. Both motors should be spinning. (See Figure 9.)

What do you notice immediately? Do two motors spin as fast as one motor? The frequency, or pitch, of the sound should tell you that the motors are spinning slower. Measure the current in the new circuit. How does the current, measured in amperes, compare to the current you measured before? It should be about half the current if the two motors are identical.

Take the meter out of the circuit and complete the circuit to drive two motors. Set the meter to measure DCV. Measure the voltage drop across either of the motors. It will be about half of the voltage drop you measured when one motor was in the circuit. The battery case is still operating at approximately 6V, and that voltage is being expended to power two motors. The voltage drop across the two motors will equal the battery voltage (measured, not necessarily the voltage listed on the battery).

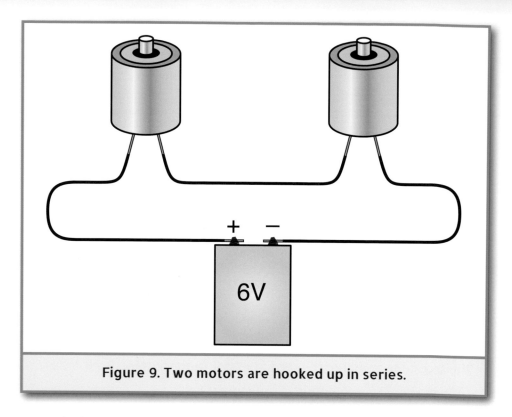

Figure 9. Two motors are hooked up in series.

The batteries output 6 volts, but the current drops in half when the load doubles. The fundamental law of electricity says that as the resistance in a circuit rises, the current decreases. This is written as:

$$V = I \times R$$

where V is the voltage, or electrical pressure; I is the current, or the quantity of electrons flowing through the circuit; and R is the resistance, a measure of how much a conductor resists the current.

Voltage is measured in volts; current is measured in amperes; and resistance is measured in ohms. All three units are named for scientists who made important discoveries about electricity. The equation illustrates Ohm's law.

One way to interpret Ohm's law is that the current flowing through a circuit is inversely proportional to the resistance in the circuit. This means that when you doubled the resistance by doubling the number of motors, the current was halved. The second circuit had twice the resistance (two motors), but the same voltage from the battery, so the current was reduced to half. You heard the difference in the hum of the motors. If you had substituted flashlight bulbs for the motors, you would have seen that the glow from each bulb was much dimmer than it would have been for one bulb.

How to Select Motors for Your Robot

You should select a motor that runs on direct current and requires less than 9 volts of DC power. For ease of operation and low cost, servos work best. Servos are specified in terms of the voltage they require, how fast they turn, and how much torque they deliver. Torque is the measure of a motor's ability to twist.

Servos powerful enough to push your small, mobile robot output approximately 3,000 g-cm or 40 oz-inches of torque. A 3,000-g-cm torque motor could lift a 3,000-gram load that is attached at a point 1 centimeter away from the shaft. Or, it could lift a load half that mass at twice the distance from the shaft. Torque is measured in units of force (grams, ounces, pounds) multiplied by distance (centimeters, inches, feet).

Servo speed is specified as rotary velocity and is measured in degrees of turns per second. A typical rotary velocity is 60 degrees every 0.22 seconds, which is the equivalent of 45 RPM.

You do not need motors of exactly this specification but something close will work well. Expect to pay ten to fifteen dollars per motor. You will need two. Check with local hobby and electronic component stores, search the Web, or order from one of the vendors listed in Appendix A. In the example robot, we use Futaba S-148 servos.

Chapter 3

HOW TO MODIFY SERVOS

Servos give powerful output motion at slow speeds that can be controlled by a computer. However, before you can use servos, you may need to modify them. Look on the servo to see if it says "Continuous rotation" or "Standard." If possible, purchase continuous rotation. If you have standard servos, this chapter will guide you in making the needed changes to them.

When you purchase standard servos, ask if there is a guide to "hacking the servo" to use in a robot. The following approach is the easiest for the Futaba S-148 servo.

Before modifying, or hacking, the servos, you should know why you are doing it. Servos were created to operate through a limited range of motion. From its center position, a standard servo may turn clockwise 180 degrees and counterclockwise 180 degrees. That limited range works well if you are using the servo to control a steering wheel on a model car or the flaps on a model airplane, but it does not help you drive a mobile robot where you want the motor to keep spinning in the same direction to move the robot. To "hack" a servo you need to eliminate the mechanisms that limit the servo's range of motion.

Converting a servo into a controllable motor takes three steps, which you will follow in Project 6. You will need to remove the piece that limits the servo's range of motion, disconnect the potentiometer to stop it from turning, and center the potentiometer shaft. Potentiometers are electronic devices that vary the resistance in a circuit as they rotate. This potentiometer tells the servo how far the shaft has rotated.

In a servo operation, as the motor turns the shaft in one direction, the potentiometer indicates how far the shaft has gone. As the potentiometer rotates, it supplies a different resistance to the circuit board. As the resistance changes, the circuit board stops the motor when the shaft has gone far enough. This is great if you want to raise and lower the antenna in your car, but for your robot, you want the motor to keep rotating and not stop. So you have to disconnect the potentiometer.

HACKING THE SERVOS

With this project, you will start to build your robot. Each subsequent project will move you one step closer to your goal of making a working robot.

If your servos look different from the one in Figure 10, consult the manufacturer's Web site for instructions on how to hack them.

This project requires a clean and uncluttered work area so you do not lose parts or damage the components of the servos. Hold the first servo with the motor shaft pointing up. Use a small Phillip's or jeweler's screwdriver to remove the four screws that hold the servo together. (See Figure 10.) Place the screws in a cup so you do not lose them.

MATERIALS

* 2 servo motors
* small Phillip's screwdriver or jeweler's screwdriver
* diagonal wire cutters
* small file or sandpaper
* safety goggles or glasses
* clean, uncluttered work area
* sheet of white paper
* cup

You can remove the bottom plate to examine the circuit board, but you must replace it. Next, carefully remove the top plate, making sure not to knock the gears loose. Look at the gears to figure out how they work. The electric motor inside the case drives the first gear, which meshes with the next gear, and so on.

Figure 10. To modify (hack) a servo motor or just to look inside, remove the four screws that hold on the top and bottom plates. Lift the gears off carefully so you can remember where they go.

Remove the middle nylon gear first. Lift it up and put it on a clean piece of paper in the same position you found it in the servo. One of the remaining two nylon gears is attached to the motor shaft that extends through the case. Leave this gear in place, and remove the other gear.

Locate the metal motor shaft and the remaining nylon gear. It sits on top of the potentiometer. Remove this gear. Looking from the top of the gear, you will see a small nylon tab sticking out from the center. In servo operation, as the shaft rotates, the tab rotates until it hits the center gear. The tab stops the motion. You need to remove the tab so the gear can continue to turn.

Put on your safety goggles, because you are about to cut off a piece that may flip toward your face. With diagonal wire cutters, and adult help if you need it, cut off the tab as close to the gear as you can.

Reassemble the gears to make sure you have cut away enough of the tab for the gears to rotate completely. If not, use a small file or sandpaper to remove the rest of the tab, being careful not to let the filings fall into the gears.

Beneath the last gear is a metal ring. Remove it and the odd-shaped plastic drive plate, which looks like a capital letter "H" with a giant hole in the center. This piece spins the potentiometer shaft when the gear spins.

Before reassembling the servo, center the potentiometer. Spin the metal shaft in one direction as far as it will go and then in the other direction to find out how far it will go. Estimate the center of its range of motion and turn it to that position. It will probably be centered when it aligns with the long axis of the servo case. Later, when you have the robot connected to your computer, you can find the center more accurately, but estimating the center position will work fine for now.

Reassemble the modified, or hacked, servo. Be careful replacing the screws. If you let the screwdriver slip out of the screw slots, you can damage the head of the screw, making it difficult to open or close the servo. Keep enough pressure on the screwdriver that you do not strip the heads of the screws. Hack the second servo in the same way you did the first servo.

Chapter 4

ADD SOME WHEELS

Once you have selected the motors for your robot, select wheels. You can make wheels from CDs, plastic sheets, or wood, or you can buy them. Wheels need to be large compared to the size of the bumps they will roll over. If the floor is littered with 2-cm– (1-in–) high obstacles, a 5-cm– (2-in–) diameter wheel (with a 2-cm or 1-in radius) will not roll over them. For smooth floors, a good wheel size to start with is 5 to 8 cm (2 to 3 in) in diameter.

Consider using plastic wheels from a baby stroller or a discarded toy. Wheels sold at hardware and garden shops for yard equipment are too heavy.

A good speed for robot movement is 5 to 10 cm (2 to 4 in) per second. A motor that spins at 45 RPM rotates ¾ of one revolution in a second. So a 5-cm– (2-in–) diameter wheel will move the robot 11.8 cm (4.7 in) in a second. The calculation starts by finding the distance the 5-cm– (2-in–) diameter wheel moves in one complete revolution:

$$\pi \times \text{diameter} = 3.14 \times 5 \text{ cm} = 15.7 \text{ cm}.$$

But at 45 RPM, the wheel rotates only ¾ of a rotation in a second, so it travels ¾ of this distance:

$$15.7 \text{ cm} \times \frac{3}{4} = 11.8 \text{ cm}.$$

Once you have selected the servo and know its speed of rotation, you can calculate the wheel size to give the speed you want the robot to move.

Arrangement of Wheels

How many wheels will you need? Since this is your robot, you can design it with as many wheels as you want, in whatever arrangement you want. Here are a few suggestions to consider.

A typical robot design uses two wheels attached to servos, or motors, and a third wheel for balance. You steer this model by adjusting the rotation of the two servos. To go forward, both wheels spin in the same direction. To turn around, one wheel goes forward, while the other spins in reverse.

In the three-wheel robot, the third wheel has to be able to turn to each side, so a caster is a good choice. You can find casters for a dollar or two at hardware stores. You need a caster that can spin as well as roll, so it can move in any direction. A ball roller will work well, too. Pass an axle through the center of a smooth ball that will roll and slip along the floor. A hallow plastic golf ball, used for practice, would make a good wheel. A third option is to use a piece of metal or plastic bent so a section touches the floor. The metal skid should slide easily in any direction. (See Figure 11.)

You are not limited to three wheels. You could use four or more. Consider using four wheels if the robot will have a heavy load or if the load will be off center. In this case, you could use two casters and two servos.

Instead of steering the robot by driving two servos at different speeds and in different directions, you could make a robot that steers like a car. Most remote control model cars have one motor

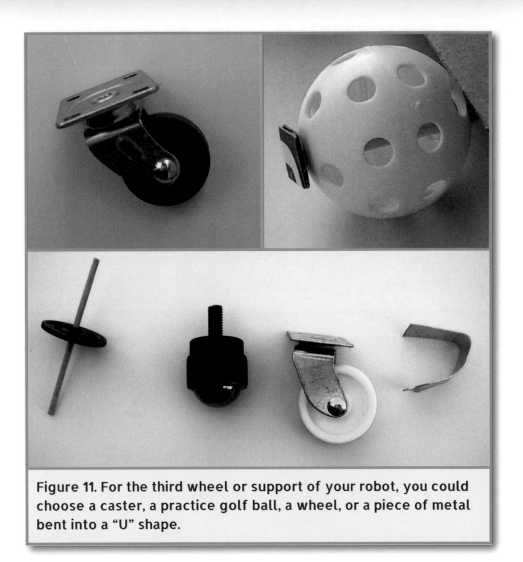

Figure 11. For the third wheel or support of your robot, you could choose a caster, a practice golf ball, a wheel, or a piece of metal bent into a "U" shape.

that drives both rear wheels on a common axle. Steering is done with a servo that rotates the front wheel or wheels. With one front wheel the design resembles a tricycle, and with two it resembles a car. Either model would be more difficult to build than the model with two driving servos and a caster.

ATTACHING THE MOTORS TO THE WHEELS

The difficulty with wheels is attaching them to the motors. The simplest drivetrain is direct drive, where the wheels are attached to the motor shaft. Ideally, you will find wheels that fit the shafts of your motors. In Project 1, you might have had to tape or glue the motor shaft to fit the driveshaft. You might have to do something similar here.

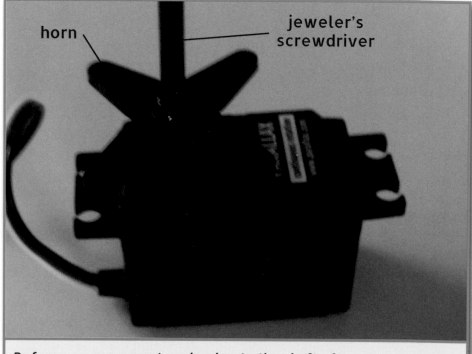

horn

jeweler's screwdriver

Before you can mount a wheel onto the shaft of a servo, you will have to remove the plastic piece called a horn. Use a jeweler's screwdriver to remove the small screw and pull up on the horn to get it off the shaft.

Try fitting a wheel onto the shaft of a servo motor. If you purchased the wheels and the motor from the same source, the wheels should fit snugly and will be held in place by the screw in the end of the servo shaft. Screw the wheel in place, making sure the surface of the wheel aligns perpendicular to the shaft. Then install the second wheel on the second servo shaft.

MATERIALS

* 2 wheels
* 2 servo motors
* plastic tubing from a hobby store
* glue
* screwdriver

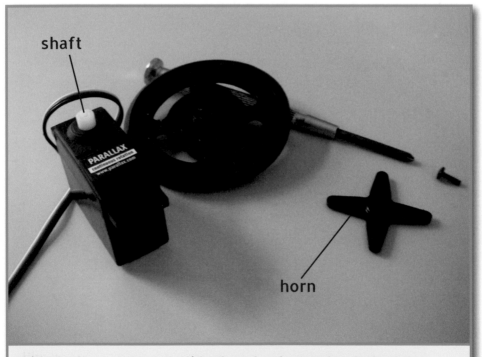

shaft

horn

With the horn removed, slide the wheel onto the shaft of the servo. Note that the wheel and shaft have grooves or splines cut into them (so the wheel doesn't slip on the shaft), so you have to get the wheel lined up carefully. Then put the screw back in.

Problems You May Encounter

If the center hole in the wheel is too small, ask an adult to enlarge the hole with a drill. Then fit the wheels onto the shafts.

A more common problem is when the wheel hole is larger than the motor shaft. One solution is to purchase plastic tubing that fits into the wheel as a bushing. Push the motor shaft into the tubing and glue it in place. If it does not fit, **get adult help** drilling out the inside of the tubing to fit the servo shaft.

Another solution uses a dowel. **Have an adult** drill a hole in the center of a section of dowel to fit onto the motor shaft. If the wheel hole is too small for the dowel, reduce the dowel's diameter by shaving it in a pencil sharpener. Put a drop of glue on each end of the dowel to hold the wheel and motor shaft.

Chapter 5

BUILD A ROBOT PLATFORM

A platform is the material to which the components attach. In a car, the frame plays the same role. The platform should be lightweight and strong and give you the ability to move components or add components.

The platform should be as small and light as possible, yet large enough to carry the components you will likely use. It needs to be strong enough not to buckle or bend under the load. You now have enough information that you can design and build the platform for your robot.

A wooden platform and metal frame carry the electronics of this robot.

BUILDING THE PLATFORM

Position the two servos and support wheels on a piece of cardboard in the configuration you want for your robot. The most common configuration is a three-wheel robot using two servos for drive wheels and a caster for support. You will attach the wheels to the bottom of the platform and, later, the microcomputer circuit board and any other components to the top, above the wheels. For stability, the wheels will have to be farther from the center of

MATERIALS

* wood (1/8- to 3/8-inch plywood)
* 2 servos with wheels attached
* caster wheel
* pencil
* cardboard
* coping saw
* carpenter's square

the platform than any significantly weighty components you place on top. If you are planning to add other components later, move the wheels outward accordingly. Check to see where the battery will go. It may be the heaviest component on the platform, so center it above the wheels. You do not want the battery tipping the robot over. Finally, see if the load on top of the platform will be balanced side-to-side and front-to-back.

When you have the wheels in position, draw a pencil line around the wheels and other components to indicate the platform size you will need. (See Figure 12.) Now you can consider both the shape and the materials you will use.

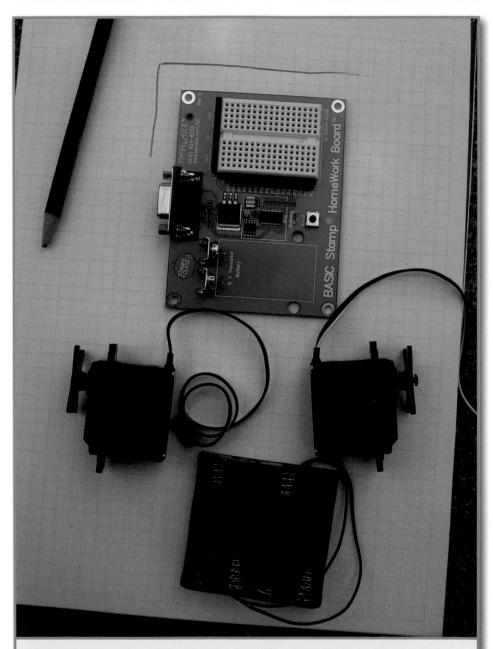

Figure 12. Lay the components on a piece of paper so you can see how they will fit together. Then take the dimensions from the paper and use them to guide you in cutting the platform. Cut the platform with a coping saw.

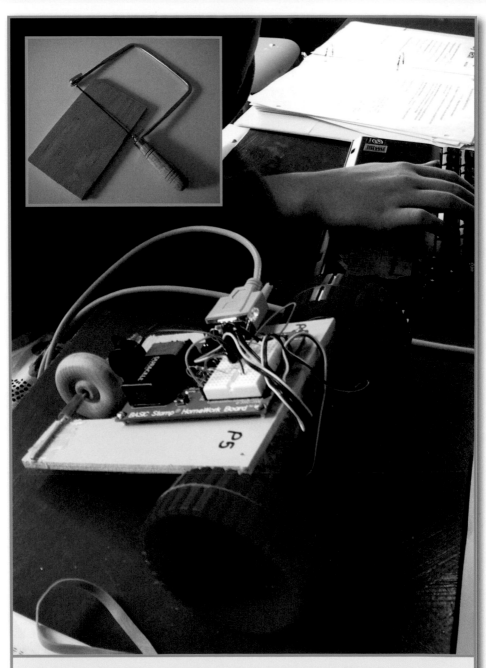

A finished model is connected to a computer so that a program can be downloaded. INSET: A coping saw is a safe way to cut the platform out of wood or plastic.

Square and rectangular shapes are easy to cut, but they waste wood and add weight at the corners that does not contribute to the robot's success. A "T" shape will allow the servos to be mounted farther apart with the load supported along the center of the robot. Think about how you will use the robot, and see if any other platform shape makes sense.

Cut the platform shape out of cardboard. Use a carpenter's square to lay out straight lines and square corners on the piece of cardboard. The outside dimensions should be roughly 12 to 18 cm (5 to 7 in) wide and 18 to 25 cm (7 to 10 in) long. Check the placement of the servos and caster again. When you have the size and shape you want in cardboard, trace its outline on plywood.

Although you can make the platform from wood, plastic, or metal, for this project use 3/8-inch plywood of grades A–A or A–C. Hardware stores and lumberyards carry this in full sheets (4 × 8 ft) and many sell it in half or quarter sheets. The platform will require a small piece of a quarter sheet of plywood.

Under adult supervision, use a coping saw to cut the plywood. This is a small, inexpensive handsaw with a thin blade that lets you cut sharp angles. After cutting out the platform, sand or remove burrs or rough spots from the cut edges.

PROJECT IDEA
AND FURTHER EXPLORATION

If you are interested in making a metal platform, check out the sheet metal and channel stock at hardware stores. Stores also carry perforated metal that will allow you to secure components with nuts and bolts. Parts from metal construction sets, like erector sets, can work as well.

Place the two servos with attached wheels on the underside of the platform. Place them on opposite sides so they are within half an inch of the ends of the platform. Measure the width of the platform and mark the center at the end opposite to the servos. Place the caster wheel here, within a half inch of the end. The three wheels should make an equilateral triangle. The height of the caster wheel, from the base to the bottom of the wheel, should be about the same as the distance from the top of a servo to the bottom of the attached wheel. This will make the platform level.

MATERIALS

* 2 servos with wheels attached
* caster wheel (from a hardware store)
* screws
* screwdriver
* pencil
* 2.5 × 5 cm (1 × 2 in) board
* robot platform
* ruler
* wood glue
* C-clamp
* drill and bits
* carpenter's square

Using a pencil, mark the holes in the base for the caster wheel. **Ask an adult** to drill small holes in the platform where you marked the holes. Screw the caster wheel into the platform.

Cut two 5-cm– (2-in–) long blocks of the 2.5 × 5 cm (1 × 2 in) board. Fit one block to one of the servos so you can mark the position of the screw holes. Repeat with the other block. **Ask an adult** to drill starter holes in these blocks of wood so you will be

A team of students run their robot along a path on the floor during the 2014 World Robot Olympiad in Sochi, Russia.

able to screw on each servo. (See Figure 13.) You are ready to attach the servos to the platform.

Place the two servos back on the underside of the platform. This is the same side that the caster wheel attaches to. Visually align the servos so they are parallel to each other and parallel to the length of the platform. Mark the location of one of the servos with a pencil. Apply wood glue to the underside of the block that is attached to the first servo. Position the servo so it is lined up with the marks you made, and clamp the block to the platform. You may need to recruit an extra pair of hands to help. If the servos are not aligned closely, operating the robot will put undue wear on the servos.

Figure 13. Use screws to attach each servo to a small block of wood. Then you can screw or glue the wood onto the underside of the platform.

When the glue has dried, apply glue to the block attached to the second servo and wheel. Before clamping it firmly to the platform, use the carpenter's square to align it with the first servo. Align one edge of the square along the edge of the first servo and align the second servo against the other side of the square. Clamp the second block and let the glue dry.

Attaching the servos in this fashion will let you unscrew them to remove them from the platform. If you glue them directly to the platform, they might break if you try to pry them off.

ATTACHING THE CIRCUIT BOARD

You will now make a riser platform to hold the circuit board. The riser platform protects the connections beneath the circuit board. Cut four 3/4-inch-long pieces of 1/2-inch dowel. Ask an adult to drill a small starter hole in the end of each section of dowel so you can screw the corners of the circuit board to the dowels. Glue the other ends of the dowels to the platform.

MATERIALS

* an adult
* robot platform
* circuit board
* 1/2-inch dowel
* screws
* drill and bits
* glue

If the circuit board does not have screw holes, attach it to the dowels with double-sided tape.

Another way to protect the circuit board connections is to mount the board by using washers beneath it.

Chapter 6

Supply Electrical Power

The voltages needed for most robots are between 1.5 volts and 12 volts DC. Batteries can supply power in this range.

Batteries convert chemical energy into electric energy. They pump electric charges from their negative terminal through the circuit to the positive terminal. The larger their rated voltage (printed on the side of the battery), the greater their ability to push electric charges through a circuit.

A D-cell battery is rated to generate 1.5 volts. That means that it could output 0.1 amps of current through a device that has 15 ohms of resistance. A 9V battery has 6 times the voltage and could push a 0.6-amp current through the same resistance.

When selecting batteries for your robot, make sure the batteries supply the correct voltages needed by the servos and microcontroller. Both come with specifications of their power requirements. Applying voltages significantly larger or smaller than those specified will probably damage the equipment or at least prevent it from working.

There are a variety of battery types on the market. The most inexpensive are the common zinc-carbon batteries. Alkaline batteries, although more expensive, are a better choice as they last several times longer. Nickel-cadmium (NiCd) batteries are rechargeable and can save money over time, but they are expensive. Also, you have to buy a charger and follow recharging procedures.

If you use rechargeable batteries, be sure to follow the directions for charging them. NiCds exhibit a memory effect. If you recharge them before they are fully drained, their capacity will diminish. So if you are going to use NiCds, have a device, like a flashlight that you can insert the batteries into so you can completely drain them before recharging.

Here are suggestions for battery care that will extend their life. Remove batteries from the circuit when you are not using them and store them in a plastic bag in the refrigerator. Do not use them directly from the refrigerator; let them warm up first. Store rechargeable batteries after they've been charged. Make sure that battery terminals are stored so that their terminals are not touching any material that conducts electricity (such as metal).

You can test the strength of a battery with a voltmeter. However, connecting a battery directly to a voltmeter might give a reading close to the rated voltage even when the battery is nearly drained. If the voltage reads under 80 percent of the rated voltage (the voltage printed on the battery), the battery is drained. A better way to test a battery is to put it in a circuit with a load. Connect the battery to one of the small electric motors you used to power the model car or boat, and measure the voltage. A nearly dead battery will have a very low voltage under a load.

If a circuit or servo requires higher voltages than the batteries you have, you can connect two or more batteries. To get 4.5 volts using AA batteries, you could connect three 1.5V batteries end to end, with positive terminals connected to negative terminals. The batteries are in a series circuit. (See Figure 14a.)

One way to make a series circuit of AA, C, or D cells is to place the batteries on two or three sheets of paper and roll them tightly together with negative terminals to positive terminals. Jam a piece of aluminum foil into each end of the roll and clip a lead to each piece of foil. You can also purchase battery holders at an electronics store.

Batteries are rated not only by the voltage they deliver, but also by the current they deliver over time. The measurement for this is the amp-hour. A battery that delivers 3 amp-hours can maintain its rated voltage while delivering 1 amp for 3 hours, or 3 amps for 1 hour. Better batteries have larger amp-hour ratings.

By connecting several batteries in a parallel circuit instead of a series circuit, you can supply the rated voltage, but increase the current available to the circuit. The voltage output will equal the voltage for each battery. A parallel circuit consists of all the positive terminals being connected together and feeding into one side of the circuit, and all the negative battery terminals being connected and feeding into the other side of the circuit. (See Figure 14b.)

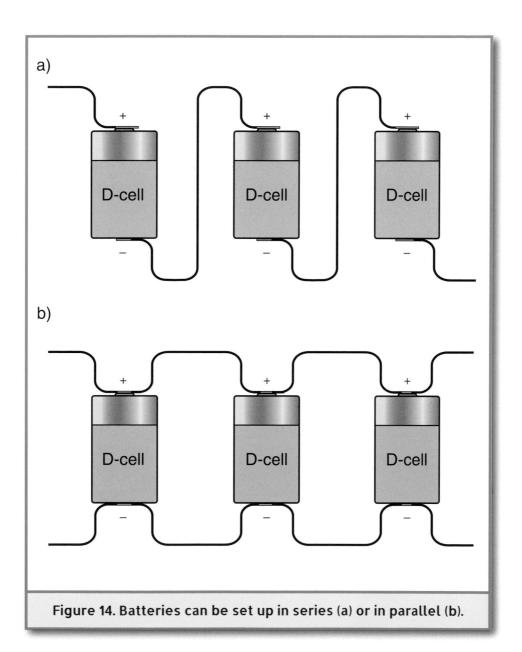

Figure 14. Batteries can be set up in series (a) or in parallel (b).

SERIES AND PARALLEL CIRCUITS

In this project you will see how the voltage differs depending on how you connect batteries.

Connect three AA batteries in a series: Line up the batteries end to end, so the middle battery's positive terminal is touching the negative terminal of one battery and its negative terminal is touching the positive terminal of the other battery. Tape the stripped end of a piece of wire to the exposed positive end of the battery pack you just made. Twist the other exposed end of the wire onto one terminal of a motor. Connect the other end of the battery pack to the other motor terminal.

MATERIALS

* 3 AA batteries
* 22-gauge wire
* voltmeter
* electric motor
* wire cutters

This pack holds four AA batteries.

Battery Basics

The letter designation of batteries is a relic from the early part of the twentieth century. When radios were first sold, they required two or three batteries of different voltages. They were designated A, B, and C, with A being the smallest and C the largest. Larger batteries for flashlights were standardized and these were called D batteries or cells. For a while, battery companies produced even larger batteries, F and G cells. Transistor radios did not require batteries as large as the older radios did. The new, smaller batteries were given the designations AA and AAA. Today there are no uses for B and A batteries since radios do not use them, so you will not find them in stores.

What can you tell by listening to the motor spin? Measure the voltage drop across the motor, as described in Project 5.

Reconnect the batteries in a parallel circuit and connect them to the motor. To do this you will need to cut and strip the ends off six short wires. Connect the positive terminals of each battery to the positive ends of the others and the negative terminals to each other. What is different about the sound made by the motor? Measure the voltage drop across the motor.

Chapter 7

CONTROL THE ROBOT'S MOTION

You can control robots either through remote control or by an onboard computer. Some robot competitions allow the use of remote control, although that falls outside our definition of a robot.

We will focus on onboard computer control. You will need to purchase a control system that you can program with your computer and that can operate the servos. Check Appendix A for a list of vendors.

The basic idea is to write a control program on a personal computer and then download it to the onboard memory in the robot's microcontroller or computer. Every time you start the robot, the small onboard computer will load and execute the program.

You can write the program in BASIC or another language (provided by the manufacturer of the microcontroller) on a personal computer. Using a wire connected to the COM port on your computer, you will send the program to the robot's microcontroller. The onboard memory, EEPROM (electrically erasable programmable read-only memory), stores the program. When you start or reset the robot, it executes the instructions saved in the EEPROM.

The EEPROM is mounted on a circuit board along with the microcontroller, power supply, and electronic components. Some

This student is connecting the servos to the Board of Education circuit board.

boards include a prototyping breadboard so you can easily wire up additional sensors (light sensors, for example), additional servos (to operate an arm), or other devices (lights). Sensors allow the robot to respond to outside stimulus, such as moving toward or away from a light or reversing when it bumps into an object. The power supply takes the voltage supplied by the batteries and converts it into the voltage required by the electronic systems on the circuit board and by the servos.

When you have the control system and have modified the servos, you will connect the servos to the circuit board and test them. Follow the directions of the control system you purchased. You will need to connect the three wires of each servo to the microcontroller. The white servo wire controls the servo; it carries the encoded signal from the control circuit to the servo. The black wires will connect to the system ground, and the red wires will connect to the input voltage, the plus side of the battery.

Remote Control

Radio (or infrared) controllers are the common method of remote control, like R/C cars, although control by wire is simpler. Hobby stores carry R/C controllers in a wide range of prices. You can purchase servos that work with the controller and make a remote-controlled boat or car. Or, you can take apart a working R/C car and use the motors and controls in a new model that you build. For detailed instructions, see the author's book *Radio-Controlled Car Experiments.* If you have an R/C car that does not work, take it apart to see how it is assembled and to find parts you might use in robot projects. As much fun as R/C models are, they are not robots and do not lend themselves to the wide range of tasks that a robot can undertake.

You can operate the robot you build with a universal remote control for a television. This becomes a remote control device rather than an autonomous robot.

In this example we are using the Stamp II microcontroller mounted on a Board of Education (BOE) circuit board made by Parallax. The board includes a breadboard, which is the white rectangle of plastic that allows you to wire circuits without soldering. (See Figure 15.) An advantage of using the breadboard is that it has internal connections. Slots that are in a row are all connected. So you could connect several components to each other by plugging them into the slots in one row.

MATERIALS

* Stamp II microcontroller
* Board of Education circuit board
* servos
* jumper wires
* 9V battery or 4 AA batteries and a battery case

You can use the breadboard to connect the servos to the control circuit, ground, and electrical power. However the BOE has dedicated slots to make the connections easier. (See Figure 16.) Without the slots you need to connect each of the three wires for each servo to a hole in a separate row of the breadboard. Then run a short wire from holes in each of the three rows to the appropriate location on the board. Insert the other end of each wire into the desired slot, for either an input/output pin, ground, or power. As you can image, the wiring for two servo connections can become messy. It is best to use the dedicated slots for servos.

Regardless of whether you wire the servos through the breadboard or through the dedicated slots, the white wire of each servo will connect to an input/output pin on the STAMP chip. The dedicated slots allow you to connect to pin numbers 12 through 15. For this example we'll use pin #15. This slot connects within the circuit board (you can't see the connection) on the BOE to the #15 input/output pin of the microcontroller STAMP chip. So the signal coming out of the STAMP chip at P15 will direct the movement of that servo. The other servo has to connect to a different pin (otherwise both servos would follow the same instructions); we'll use #14.

The red wire of each servo will connect through the slot to the positive side of the power supply (Vin) and the black wires will connect to the ground (Vss). Vss is the power-supply ground, which represents the negative side of the batteries.

Connect the cable Parallax provides to a USB slot of a personal computer and connect the other end to the port on the circuit

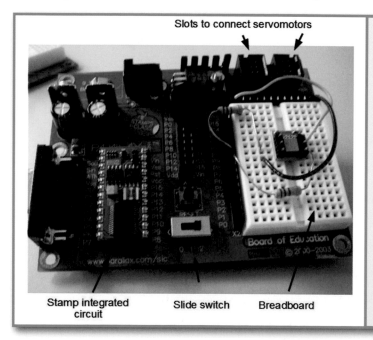

Slots to connect servomotors

Stamp integrated circuit   Slide switch   Breadboard

Figure 15. Here is the layout of the Board of Education circuit board. The white breadboard allows you to quickly wire circuits. The STAMP chip is the micropro-cessor or computer on board the robot.

Figure 16. Connect each servo to one of the servo ports on the top of the Board of Education.

board. Use either a 9V battery or 4 AA batteries in a battery case that plugs into the barrel slot on the BOE.

Older BOEs have a tiny LED that will light up once power is inserted. Newer boards have a switch at the bottom that helps save power. When you slide the switch from position 0 (off) to position 1 (programing), a tiny LED flashes. The third position (2) provides power to the servos. You can use position 1 to program the robot and to run programs, but the servos won't move until you slide the switch to position 2.

Remember when you modified the servos, you learned that there is an accurate way to center the potentiometer. Now that you have wired the circuit board, you are almost ready to do this. First, however, you have to install the software in your computer. Download the software from the Parallax website (parallax.com) for free. Go to the Support tab and click on Downloads. Select the Basic Stamp Editor.

Writing a Computer Program for Your Robot

The beauty of a robot is that you can write a program on a computer, download the program to the robot, and have the robot execute each step. So far you have prepared the drive system and connected it to the control circuit. Now you are ready to write a simple program to rotate the wheels.

The first program to try is to get each servo to rotate. This will allow you to make sure the potentiometers are centered. You will want to send a series of electric pulses to each servo. You will have to tell the microcontroller where the servos are connected (what the output pin number is). You will also have to specify the pulse width of the signal. Electronics inside the servo will interpret the pulse width as a command to rotate in one direction or the other, or to not rotate at all. You need to know what pulse width directs no motion, so you know what values to use for forward and backward motion.

Write a simple program to rotate one servo at a time, following the example in the next project. Record which direction each servo rotates at different pulse widths and find the pulse width value that gives no motion. Keep this information, along with any programs you write and your design ideas, in a notebook.

Experiment 13

Running Servos with a Stamp Chip

To run the Stamp software, you need to download the software from a manufactures site and install it on your computer. See the Web site on the previous page.

Once the Basic Stamp Editor is installed, open the editor. Follow the instructions on the figure below.

Then enter the following code:

```
'Program to test servos
center:
pulsout 15, 750
pause 20
goto center
end
```

MATERIALS

* personal computer
* Basic Stamp Editor
* robot with control board and servos
* USB connector
* battery (9V) or 4 AA batteries in a battery case

Under the File tab, find Save to keep the program. Let's call it Test1. Connect the battery or battery case to the BOE and turn the switch to position 1. On your computer, click on the triangle to run the program.

The computer will run a diagnostic test on the code to see if you made any typing errors. If you did not, the computer will send the program to the robot. Immediately it will start executing the program.

If everything is working, nothing will happen. Slide the switch to position 2 so the servo can now execute the command. Push the reset button that is directly above the slide switch. The servo should move.

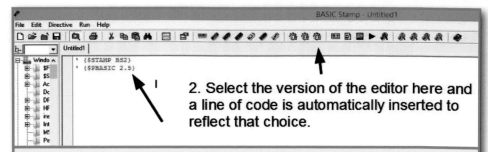

2. Select the version of the editor here and a line of code is automatically inserted to reflect that choice.

With the editor program running on your computer, the first step is to tell the program which of the three editors you will use. Select the latest version, the one on the far right. As soon as you click on one, a line of code will pop up in the program reflecting your choice.

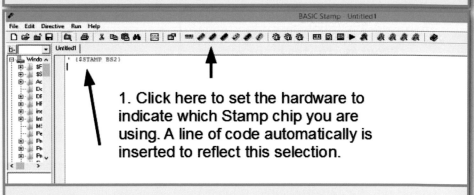

1. Click here to set the hardware to indicate which Stamp chip you are using. A line of code automatically is inserted to reflect this selection.

Now tell the computer which set of hardware you are using. In this example it is BS2. Again a line of code will automatically enter your program reflecting this choice.

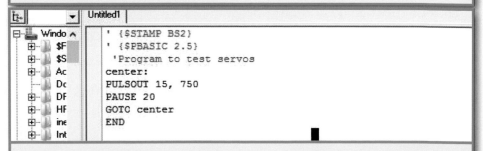

Enter the program as it is written here. Remember that computers do what you tell them to do; they don't necessarily do what you want them to do. Make sure you have entered the code correctly.

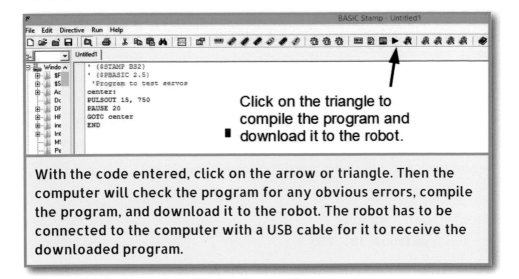

Click on the triangle to compile the program and download it to the robot.

With the code entered, click on the arrow or triangle. Then the computer will check the program for any obvious errors, compile the program, and download it to the robot. The robot has to be connected to the computer with a USB cable for it to receive the downloaded program.

This program told the servo to move to position 750. If 750 is the center position for this servo, it wouldn't move. More than likely, it did move and still is moving. Slide the switch to position 1 so the servo stops moving.

You'd like to know where exactly the center position is. Numbers higher than the center position will move the robot in one direction; lower numbers will move it in the opposite direction. Therefore, it is important to know the center.

Run the program again. Slide the switch to position 2. The robot has stored the program in its memory (EEPROM) so you don't have to download it again from your computer. Which way is the servo spinning? If you had shut the power off, the program will stop. To relaunch it, push the reset button.

Now change the program by using a number different than 750. Try 800. Download the program and run it. Does the servo spin in the same direction? Try 700. You want to find a position where the servo spins in the opposite direction. Once you've located that, find the position where the servo does not move at all. This is the center.

Record this number. Write it on a piece of masking tape and tape it to the side of the servo.

Some servos have a tiny opening in the side where you can manually adjust the servo. If your servos have this feature, use a jeweler's screwdriver to rotate the tiny screw inside the opening while running the first program. By twisting the screwdriver back and forth you will find a position where it doesn't spin.

Now test the other servo. Change the program to operate the other servo. Instead of

```
pulsout 15, 750
```

insert

```
pulsout 14, 750
```

This will send the electric pulses to the pin (#14) where the second servo is connected. Repeat the process for finding the center of this servo.

You have to do this procedure only once for each servo. By recording the center value or by manually centering the servo you are set to use the servos in other programs.

Understand the Program

The program you just used tells the microcontroller to send a pulse that is 750 time units long to the servo number 14 or 15. Each unit is 2 microseconds long; so the total width of the pulse is 750 times 2 microseconds, which is 1.5 milliseconds. (A microsecond is a millionth of a second, and a millisecond is a thousandth of a second.)

Assuming that the servo is centered, if it receives a pulsout command of 750 it will not turn. If the pulsout signal is larger, say 850, it will spin in one direction. Smaller values, say 650, will spin it in the other direction.

This is how we control the motion of the robot. We send signals to the servos and the pulse width of the signals determines how fast the servo will turn and in what direction. This method of controlling servos is called *pulse width modulation*.

The other commands in the computer program caused a 20-millisecond pause before repeating the pulsout command. Servos need time to reset after every operation, so a 20-millisecond pause is inserted.

The goto center command directs the robot to look for a place in the program called "center." It knows that "center" is a place because the name is followed by a colon.

Once back at the beginning of the program it ran it again, and again, until you cut the power.

Since there was nothing in the program to stop it, it continued until you pulled the battery out.

So far you have learned how servos work and how to modify them, how to control them with pulse width modulation, how to write a BASIC program, and how to wire a breadboard. Those are the essential skills you need to make your robot do whatever you want. It is time to move on to programming the platform to execute complicated movements.

Problems You Might Encounter

If the program fails to execute, it will provide a reason. Make a change to the program and try it again. The most frequent problem is that the batteries lose their charge and the robot either stops working or acts in unpredictable ways.

Project 14

MOVING THE ROBOT IN A STRAIGHT LINE

In autonomous operation a robot follows a set of instructions you have programmed. The instructions are stored in an onboard memory, or EEPROM. Each time you start the robot it will move through the sequence of steps you programmed.

On a smooth floor, lay down a strip of tape that is one yard long. Now, program your robot to travel along the tape and stop at the end. It may take a few tries to complete this challenge. Keep notes of the program you use and of the values of the variables in the program.

The program you write must take into account that the two servos will rotate in different directions. If you have mounted the servos so the wheels are on the outboard sides of the robot, they are facing opposite directions. The servo on the left side is pointing to the left, while the other servo is pointing to the right. If you programmed each to rotate clockwise, one will rotate its wheel to move the robot forward and the other will rotate its wheel backward. To move the robot forward requires one wheel to spin clockwise and the other to spin counterclockwise.

When you have managed to get the robot to move along the tape and stop at the end, record the values you used in the program. Knowing how many pulses are required to move one yard will make it easier for you to program the robot for new challenges.

Here is a sample program to use:

```
'Running a straight line
x       var    word
leftservo       con   15
rightservo      con   14
forward:
for x=1 to 400
        pulsout leftservo, 650
        pulsout rightservo, 850
next
end
```

The first line of code starts with an apostrophe. This signals the robot that it should not try to execute whatever follows the apostrophe. This is the name of the program. You can include any notes to yourself that will make it easier to remember six months from now what the program does or how it does it.

The second line sets "x" as a variable requiring the memory space of a "word." You can put any number into this space as long as the number isn't bigger than the space. "Word" allows numbers up to 65,535, which is much larger than you will need now.

The next two lines in the program assign the name "leftservo" to input/output pin 15 and "rightservo" to input/output pin 14. You might it easier to use words like "leftservo" instead of the servo number.

"Forward" is a place in the program just like "center" was a location in the first program. The code under the name "forward" directs the onboard computer to send an electric pulse to the left servo that is 650 time units long, and a pulse of 850 time units to the right servo. Each time unit is 2 microseconds, so the first command represents 1,300 microseconds or 1.3 milliseconds.

The circuit board in the servo will interpret that signal as an order to rotate the shaft counterclockwise.

If the pulsout time had been 750, or 1.5 milliseconds, the circuit board would have directed the motor not to move at all (assuming the servo was centered at 750). Values greater than 750 will cause a servo to rotate in the clockwise direction.

The pulsout command for the right servo is 850. Thus, the right servo is 100 units above center, 750, and the left servo is 100 below 750, so the motors will rotate in opposite directions to move the robot forward.

The two servos should rotate at about the same speed, but you may notice the robot drifting to one side or the other. If this happens, you will need to speed up one servo or slow down the other. The farther the rotation number is from 750, the faster the servo will turn. However do not use values greater than 900 or less than 600 to prevent damage to the servo.

The "next" command tells the computer to go back to the start of this loop, increase the value of x by 1, and repeat the steps. It will continue to loop until it has executed the loop 400 times. When it gets to 401, it will skip the loop and move down to the instructions in the program below "next." That is "end."

Problems You Might Encounter

If the robot did not move in a straight line, the two servos might not be spinning at the same rate or the wheels might not be aligned. It is also possible that the caster is not spinning freely.

Check the wheel alignment first. You should be able to see any major misalignment by looking at the wheels and servos. Are the wheels parallel to each other and aligned with the platform? Then check the caster to ensure that it can turn freely.

See if your servos have a tiny hole in one side with a screw visible. If they do, you can adjust the center value of your servos by using a jeweler's screwdriver.

Also watch the wheels to see if they wobble as the robot moves. They might not be squarely mounted on the servo shaft.

If you suspect that the servos are operating at different speeds, make adjustments to one and rerun the program. Record the rotation numbers that work best to move your robot forward.

Making the Robot Turn

How will you get the robot to turn? You have choices. You could make a left turn by moving the right wheel forward or moving the left wheel backward. Or, to make a tighter turn, you could move the right wheel forward and the left wheel backward at the same time.

Experiment with your robot to find the values that will give a crisp turn to the left and right. Record these values in your notebook so you can use them whenever you want to execute a turn.

To make the robot move forward, you used a rotation value for one servo that was larger than the center value and a value for the other that was smaller. To get the robot to turn, both values will likely be either greater or smaller than the center value. To move the robot backward, the values for the two servos will be switched from the values used to drive it forward.

Project 15

COMPLETING THE SQUARE

When you have gotten your robot to move in a straight line and turn, write a program to get it to travel a square and end up where it started.

Start with the strip of tape you laid on the floor before and complete a square with tape. Combine the program for moving straight with the program for making a left turn and repeat the commands to complete a square. The challenge is to get the robot to stop exactly where it started after moving around the square. It will take several tries to get the right values for the time units. Record this program.

After you get the robot to complete the square, look at the code you wrote. That's a lot of lines of code. Can you simplify it?

Remember that when we wanted to send many pulses to each servo, we did not write the pulsout command over and over again. We programmed the computer to repeat the process. That is the same thing we want to do here. We want the robot to move forward 1 m (1 yd), turn, and repeat that three more times.

Since the program is already using the variable x, you can't use that. Introduce a new variable, y, and create a second loop. This loop needs a "next" command at its end to tell the computer to go back up and repeat itself. Give this a try and see how many lines of code you can eliminate while getting the robot to run a square.

Chapter 8

WHAT ELSE CAN THE ROBOT DO?

You have mastered the basics of robot building, and now you can set your sights on doing much more. The next level of complexity in building a robot is adding sensors to control the motion. Each input/output (I/O) pin on the circuit board can control a sensor or other device. At this point, you have used two I/O pins to control two devices, the left and right servos.

Sensors allow the robot to collect information, make decisions based on the program you have provided, and take action. An example of a robot sensor is a device that can detect light. You could add light detectors to your robot and program it to move toward or away from a light source.

Bump sensors detect contact with an object and close switches that send signals to the robot. These switches are often used to interrupt electrical power to the servos to stop the robot. A common challenge for an amateur robot builder is

This microswitch can be used to make a bump or touch sensor. You can find these at electronics stores.

to program a robot to run through a maze. With bump sensors a robot can be programmed to stop, turn in one direction, and then move forward until it bumps into the next wall.

Before covering sensors and arms, we present some background information on electronics components you will need.

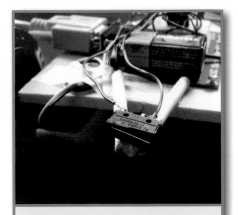

The microswitch installed on the front of this robot can tell the robot if it has run into an object.

The Whistler Bot has two touch sensors installed.

Robotic arms use sensors and motors to grab and lift objects.

Electronics Basics

Electronics is the study and application of devices to control the flow of electricity to do specific jobs. There are many different types of devices, and we introduce here the principal ones you will use.

The most basic component is the resistor. Resistors oppose the flow of electricity, or the current. They are made of two leads connected by a material that conducts electricity poorly.

Does it seem odd that we would want to resist the flow? Resistors can protect other components from receiving too much current, or voltage. They can adjust the current to get the optimum flow. Working in circuits with other devices, resistors make the current behave differently. Resistors come in a wide range of sizes that are specified by their resistance, measured in ohms.

Capacitors

In a 1-volt circuit, a capacitor of 1-farad capacitance would hold 6.28×10^{18} electrons.

Remember Ohm's law? It states that the voltage in a circuit is equal to the current times the resistance. In a circuit that has a resistor connected to a battery, the current will change if we change the resistor. If the battery supplies 1 volt and the resistor has 1 ohm, the current will be 1 ampere. Increase the resistance (the ohms of the resistor), and the current will decrease.

To change the resistance in a circuit, you can add other resistors in a series (end to end) or use a potentiometer. Potentiometers, like the ones inside servos, are devices that can have different resistances depending on the position of the shaft.

Capacitors store electrons. Think of a capacitor as having two sheets of metal foil separated by a sheet of paper. If you connected each metal sheet to opposite ends of a battery, the battery would add electric charges to each. However, the paper between them would block the flow of electricity, so there would be no current. The charges on the two metal sheets could supply power to another device. For example, if you disconnected the battery and replaced it with a resistor, current would flow through the resistor. The capacitor stored energy, although only briefly.

Because capacitors can store energy you need to be careful in handling them. Capacitors are used to store energy for strobes and flash devices in photography, and these capacitors store enough energy to cause a painful shock. Avoid making contact with the leads of capacitors.

Capacitors are described by the maximum electric charge (capacitance) they can hold and by the voltage for which they are designed. The unit of capacitance is a farad. In robots most capacitors are rated for a tiny fraction of a farad and are specified in terms of microfarads, or millionths of a farad.

The most interesting group of components is semiconductors. Wires and metals, in general, conduct electricity. Many other materials, like glass and paper, do not. Semiconductors act like both conductors and nonconductors. The principle component of semiconductors is silicon. By itself silicon is a nonconductor. But when combined with other elements, silicon can share electrons with the other material, thus allowing current to flow. Combining two different types of materials in one device allows current to flow in one direction but not the other. This device is called a diode.

There are two special types of diodes: light-emitting diodes and photodiodes. Light-emitting diodes, LEDs, are tiny sources of light. You may want to add LEDs to your circuits to indicate when power is going to a servo. LEDs can produce either visible or infrared light. Photodiodes can be used to detect light.

One of the most important inventions of the twentieth century is the transistor. It is a semiconductor device that can amplify electrical signals. Transistors have three connectors: a base, an emitter, and a collector. Current enters through the emitter and leaves through the collector. The base supplies a signal that is amplified and output from the collector. Radios have amplifiers made of transistors, so the weak signal received from the radio station can be amplified into a booming sound. You can easily damage transistors with heat (from a soldering iron) or electricity. (Make sure that you are connecting transistors according to the circuit diagram.)

Another type of semiconductor is a photo-resistor. The electrical resistance of this device depends on how much light hits it. It has high resistance when there is no light shining on it and low resistance when light strikes it. Using photo-resistors, you could build a robot that moves toward or away from a source of light. Such a robot could play hide-and-seek, moving throughout a room until it found a dark place to hide.

Integrated circuits are tiny circuits that combine the various components into a device to do specific tasks. If you open up a computer or other electronic device you will see rectangular blocks with multiple leads that are connected to other components or integrated circuits (ICs). The technology for making ICs has advanced so quickly that electronics companies are continuously creating new products and smaller versions of older products. In your robot, the microcontroller is an integrated circuit connected to I/O pins and other components.

To be able to control a robot with a computer requires the robot to have digital circuits. The model car and boat you built are analog circuits; if you increased the voltage of the battery (by using a larger battery), the DC motor would spin faster and the car or boat would move faster.

A digital circuit is one in which electric currents are on or off. Computers are huge digital circuits with each keystroke or command transformed into a string of on-and-off commands, or ones and zeros. Using computers to control servos lets you create programs with intricate moves or responses to sensors. For example, a program could tell the robot to move forward until it bumps into an object, then stop, back up, turn to the right, and start forward again. Digital circuits control servos by sending pulses of electricity through the third (white) wire.

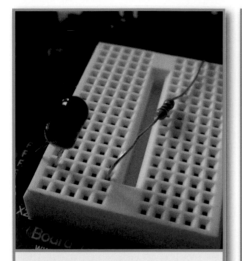

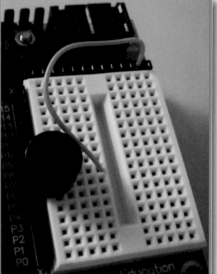

To connect an LED to the breadboard, it has to be connected in series with a resistor to prevent damage to the LED and the robot.

To make sounds, add a Piezo speaker. This one is wired into the breadboard.

This robot navigates using infrared sensors. The two objects that look like eyes are infrared LEDs that send out pulses of invisible light.

Applications

With this limited background you can search for designs of simple circuits to add to your robot and purchase components to build them. A simple addition for your robot would be to add a bump switch.

Bump switches detect physical contact. When the robot bumps into something, the moveable arm depresses and closes a switch. This sends an electric pulse to the microcontroller. The program could instruct the microcontroller to stop the servos or reverse their directions when the front bump switch is triggered. You could have several bump switches, each generating a different set of commands to move the robot away from obstacles.

To make a bump switch you need a spring-mounted switch. You can make one or purchase one at an electronics store. You also need a 10K-ohm resistor. Connect one side of the switch to the circuit ground. Connect the other side of the switch both to one side of the resistor and to a pin on the microcontroller. The other side of the resistor connects to the positive voltage supply (+5 volts). When the switch is open (not bumped), the pin is exposed to +5 volts. When the switch is bumped, the circuit closes, current flows, and the input pin senses low voltage. The computer program would specify what the input pin number is and what action to take when the pulse is sent to that pin. The resistor keeps the current low enough so it does not damage the microcontroller.

Instead of waiting until the robot makes contact with something, you could add different sensors that see objects, bounce sound waves off objects, or measure temperature. Simple circuits can direct the robot toward or away from light sources using photo-resistors. Two photo-resistors on opposite sides of the robot can steer it; when one receives more light from a source than the other, it directs the servo on the opposite side to move forward. This steers the robot toward the light. When both photo-resistor circuits sense equivalent light levels, they direct both servos forward.

Sonar transducers convert sound into electrical signals and can warn the robot that it is approaching an object. Infrared sensors, photo-resistors that detect light at infrared wavelengths, can sense temperature. Local robot groups (see Appendix B) can help you find both the sensors and circuit diagrams to add capabilities to your robot. Also, search the Internet for circuit diagrams and descriptions.

Robotic Arms

If you imagine your hand is the gripper of a robotic arm, you can appreciate how complex it is to grasp an object. When you can see the object you want to pick up, your brain controls the many muscles in your shoulder, arm, and hand to move toward the object. You correct or redirect the motion based on seeing the hand move toward it. Without sight you might be able to pick it up, but only because you have experienced the task thousands of times. In addition to sight, you rely on your sense of touch to let you know whether you are touching it.

Once you have grasped the object and contracted your fingers around it—not so tightly that it will break and not so loosely that it will slip away—your muscles pull it toward you. Muscles in your wrist may rotate your hand so you can see the object better, while muscles in your upper arm contract to bring your wrist closer, and muscles in your shoulder and chest rotate your arm toward the center of your body.

In addition to making mobile or moving robots, you can build robotic arms to throw objects or move things.

Consider how difficult the same task would be for a robot. Remembering how many lines of computer code it took to get your robot to roll in a straight line, imagine what would be involved in writing the code to pick up a simple object. Think of all the different muscles involved and how difficult it would be to replace each with a motor.

It is possible to build a fully articulated arm—an arm that can move in any direction—but it is difficult. In most cases it is easier to design a simple device to do the task you want the robot to accomplish, rather than building a general purpose, fully articulated arm. For example, if the task is to pick up Ping-Pong balls that are lying on the floor, you could add a suction hose attached to a vacuum cleaner, a static arm with sticky tape attached to it, a continuously rotating wheel that spins the balls into a basket (like the circular broom on a street sweeper), or a scoop that attaches to the front of the robot (like a front-end loader or bulldozer). Any would be easier to build and operate than a full arm.

If you are intent on building a full arm, consider starting with a toy robot arm or construction set. You may be able to control the arm structure and motors with the onboard microcontroller or with a separate remote control.

Starting from scratch you could create an arm based on any of several different models. Using a steam shovel as a model, the arm could rotate around its base, raise or lower its upper and lower parts, and raise or lower a bucket or hook that is attached to the far end of the lower arm. Other models to consider are a front-end loader, a backhoe, and a high-rise crane. For the crane, the arm rotates in a plane parallel to the ground, without moving up and down. A device moves in and out along the arm and that device reels in or lets out cable to raise or lower the load.

Before starting to build a full arm, consider whether a limited function arm will suffice; it will be much easier to build and operate. Try several different designs and make mock-ups of each to test them. When you find the arm that works best for a specific application, decide how to attach it to the robot platform. If the arm and the load it moves have any significant mass, you may have to redesign the platform to keep it from tipping over. Operating the arm will place a great drain on your battery, so you may need to add batteries. If the arm and load are too massive, the servos driving the mobile robot may not be adequate and will need upgrading.

Chapter 9

ROBOT COMPETITIONS AND SCIENCE FAIR PROJECTS

Designing and building a robot is not only fun, but it can provide the start of an award-winning project for a science fair, invention contest, or robot competition. Each event will have specific criteria for entry and rules that you need to comply with.

Most robot contests involve competing with other robots. The most basic is a sumo tournament in which two robots try to push each other out of a circle. More complex events include fire fighting, vacuum cleaning, and playing soccer.

A robot you design and build could be an ideal entry for an invention contest. The robot will have to be able to do some task, specified by the contest rules or selected by you. Just having a robot that moves would not be a strong contest entry, but if it picks up paper clips and staples with a magnet it might be.

Many schools hold science fairs, and a robot you built would impress the judges. For a great science fair project, you will need to design an experiment that allows you to test the robot and collect and analyze numerical data, since projects are judged in part on data collection and analysis. Here are some suggestions for projects.

The World Robot Olympiad is hosted by a new country each year. Students from around the globe develop their creativity, design, and problem-solving skills through competition and activities.

Science Fair Project Ideas

If you are using servos on your robot, you could compare the pulse widths (numerical values used in the pulsout commands) to the rotational speed of the motor shaft or wheels in revolutions per minute. For the servos described earlier, a pulse of 750 time units did not rotate the shaft. Pulses longer than 750 rotated it in one direction, and pulses shorter rotated it in the other direction. You could collect and graph data of the shaft speed in RPMs at different pulse widths. For pulses more than 100 units away from the center (750 in this case), the rotational speed has little variation, so most of the interesting data will be with 100 units on either side of the center. You could convert the graph of the data into speed of the robot; in this form the data can be helpful to you in determining pulsout values to use in writing programs.

Adding a bump sensor empowers a robot to find its way through a maze. An interesting project would be to build a maze and evaluate different strategies for getting the robot through the maze. For example, a simple strategy is to have the robot turn right whenever it bumps into a wall. After programming that strategy into the robot, time the robot as it makes it way through the maze. You would need to make at least three trials with each program to see if the resulting times are consistent. Then try different strategies and report on the strategies and explain why one worked better than others.

With light-detecting sensors on the robot you could run several experiments. You could test how the type of light or the lighting conditions changed the performance of the robot. You could also change the hardware (the type of light sensors or how they are mounted on the platform) or software to see how each affected the robot's performance.

If you do not have an experimental plan that appeals to you, show your robot to your science teacher or to local robot hobbyists (see Appendix C for a list of clubs) and enlist their help.

Robot Competitions

Robot competitions occur around the United States and throughout the world. You can find events near your home. A visit to a competition will excite you about building your own robot and will help you understand the technology and products available.

You might be interested in entering a competition, either by yourself or with a few friends. You will find the experience richly rewarding.

Note that not all of the following competitions ask you to build autonomous robots. Some challenge you to build robot-like devices or remote controlled machines. These all are great activities and wonderful ways to learn.

The following section lists some of the largest competitions available for you to enter.

Events for Students

BEST is one of the longest-running robot events in the United States. BEST stands for boosting engineering, science, and technology. It is a school-based event where a challenge is issued each year and teams have several weeks to decide how to meet the challenge by building mechanical devices.

Do a search for "BEST Robotics" or go to Wikipedia to find out whether your state has a participating group and how you can get involved.

The Botball Educational Robotics Program has middle school and high school students working in teams to build autonomous robots.

FIRST is a nonprofit organization that runs a series of competitions for different age groups. For elementary school students, it works with LEGO to field the FIRST LEGO League, possibly the best known of the robotic competitions. For even younger kids, it has the noncompetitive Junior FIRST LEGO League. It operates the FIRST Robotics Competition for high school students.

IEEE Micromouse Maze competitions challenge students to make robots that run a maze and compete for fastest times. These events are held throughout the world.

RoboCup is an international competition in which robots play soccer. The official name for the competition is Robot Soccer World Cup. Can you imagine making a robot that plays soccer? Check this out.

RoboFest is run by Lawrence Technology University and includes events for students in grades four through college.

RoboRAVE International operates in New Mexico and offers events for several different age groups.

Trinity College Robot Contests includes events for several age groups. Their signature event is the Fire Fighting Home Robot Contest where a robot must navigate through a model home, find a burning candle, and extinguish it. In another event a robot must pick up a plate of food, find its way through a maze, and deliver the food to a hungry person.

VEX Robotics Competition is an event for students ages 11–18. It presents a new problem for teams to solve each year.

World Robot Olympiad is an international competition for elementary, junior high, and high school students. They use LEGO Mindstorms equipment. The event is held in different countries every year.

Other Types of Events

The number of robotic and robot-like competitions for students has grown tremendously in recent years. Some are geared to students and others are for university-level students or professional robot engineers.

Each year, news media cover the DARPA Challenge, which has teams build autonomous automobiles and drive them long distances. Several other organizations sponsor similar competitions.

Duke University holds an annual wall-climbing competition for robots. The robots are judged on their ability to quickly carry something up a wall while avoiding obstacles.

Imagine how difficult it is to build a robot that operates on dry land; making an autonomous submarine is much more challenging! The AUVSI Foundation and the US Navy's Office of Naval Research sponsor these competitions.

Only slightly less challenging is MATE's (Marine Advanced Technology Education) remotely operated vehicle (ROV) competition. If this appeals to you, search for MATE's ROV building classes.

If there are underwater robots, there must be robots that fly. And there are competitions to see which team can build the flying robot that best meets the challenge. The International Aerial Robotics Competition is for university students, but if you check it out, you can start getting your future designs ready now.

ROBOT KITS AND SUPPLIES

The advantage of using robot kits is that the components are selected to work together. The wheels should fit easily onto the servos and the controls are designed to operate the servos. The disadvantage of using kits is that you are locked into the system that the kit manufacturer uses. If you start with a LEGO kit, you will have to use LEGO components because no other components will fit.

You have much greater flexibility and room for growth when you order the components separately. However, you also have a much greater chance of purchasing incompatible components. Learning how to select compatible components is an important skill, but it can be frustrating.

Here are some of the many types of kits and sources for components.

Arduino

Arduino is an open source system with easy to use hardware and software. It has become very popular in the last few years and many vendors sell their products. Wikipedia has a great page of information on Arduino.

arduino.cc

Arrick Robotics

Arrick Robotics is full of good information and products.

arrickrobotics.com

BASICX

This is a source for microcontrollers, the brains used in robots.

basicx.com

Ezrobots

This site offers several systems for building some fancy robots.

ez-robot.com

Futaba

For remote control systems and servos, contact Futaba.

futaba-rc.com

Gleason Research

This company sells several controllers and components.

gleasonresearch.com/products.phtml

Handy Board

This company offers two different platforms. One is the venerable Handy board. It is a microcontroller system that lets you build mobile robots for educational, hobbyist, and industrial purposes. They also sell the Cricket, a tiny computer you can program using Logo. Cricket would be a good choice for your first robot as it is geared for the younger robot builder.

handyboard.com

Herbach and Rademan

They offer a wide assortment of products for science and industry from their catalog and Web site.

herbach.com

Jameco

This company sells electronic components and motors through its catalog.

jameco.com

Visit their robot store at **jameco.com/Jameco/robot/robotstore. html**

Kelvin Educational

Kelvin supplies materials for a variety of educational products, including motors, wheels, gears, wire and electrical components. It also carries remote control and robot kits.

kelvin.com

K'Nex

K'Nex offers an assortment of construction kits, including some that allow computer control.

knex.com

LEGO Mindstorms

This is the most popular robot kit. It has the advantages of compatibility with existing LEGO building systems, clear instructions, and ease of use.

Mindstorms includes a computerized brick, motors, sensors, and software to run on a PC. Because it is affordable and popular, Mindstorms competitions and classes are offered throughout the United States. Computer instructions are transmitted to the robot by an infrared beam. LEGO claims that, "A first-time user with basic PC skills can design, program, and build a simple robot within one hour."

mindstorms.lego.com

Lynxmotion, Inc.

Lynxmotion is one of the oldest manufacturers of robot kits, including robot arms, biped walking robots, quadrupeds, hexapods, tracked and wheeled vehicles, and more. They are the home of the modular robotic building system called the Servo Erector System.

lynxmotion.com

Mekatronix

Mekatronix makes autonomous mobile robots, robot kits, microcontroller kits, and robot accessories, as well as educational materials related to science and robotics.

mekatronix.com

Mr. Robot

Mr. Robot distributes robot kits, microcontroller kits, microcontrollers, autonomous programmable mobile robots, software, R/C servos, gearhead DC motors, LEGO, and more.

mrrobot.com

Parallax

This company makes STAMP chips and robotic components. Their site offers a rich assortment of products and help. They have an active group of users who share information.

parallax.com

PONTECH

This company sells a variety of hardware and software products including motors, stepper motors, and servo motors.

pontech.com

Spark Fun

Spark Fun has a variety of products and help for robot builders. If you're ever in doubt about what projects might interest you, here is a site with a ton of suggestions and tutorials.

learn.sparkfun.com

Solarbotics

Solarbotics sells a variety of components and several solar-powered-robot kits. They have a rich assortment of motors and controllers.

solarbotics.com

Technology Arts

Technology Arts sells several different microcontrollers for very small robots.

technologicalarts.com

OTHER APPROACHES TO ROBOTICS

There are several other ways to get machines to move and do work. One Is BEAM. The acronym stands for Biology, Electronics, Aesthetics, and Mechanics. Instead of using digital microcontrollers, BEAM robots use analog circuits. The robots described in this book use digital control that is provided by a number-crunching computer. BEAM uses the older non-digital approach. This is certainly worth looking at.

Instead of using motors you can use wire to move components. The wires are called muscle wires. When the wires carry electricity they heat up and contract and they quickly cool and lengthen when the current is removed. This is a very clever way to make light-weight robots. Search the web for muscle wire. Here is a place to get started:

Stiquito for Beginners: An Introduction to Robotics is a book and materials to build a six-legged robot using muscle wire (wire that contracts on heating) instead of motors or servos.
Web site: **robotbooks.com/Muscle_Wires.htm**

The Playful Invention Company is a great site to visit. They don't sell anything, but they can launch you into some interesting projects. On their site check out SCRATCH. You can download it for free and use it to create your own music and animation. You will be inspired by what you see.
Web site: **playfulinvention.com**

ROBOTICS CLUBS AND ORGANIZATIONS

In addition to the robot competitions listed previously, there are many local groups that hold events and help robot builders. Do an Internet search for clubs or groups in your area. There will be some for students and others for adults. But even the adult groups might invite you to attend and participate.

Like groups of enthusiasts anywhere, robot clubs tend to be helpful and encouraging. They offer a great atmosphere for people starting out in robotics. Attend a meeting to see whether you are comfortable with the group and whether you can develop your robot-building skills with the members you meet.

FURTHER READING

Books

Baum, Dave. *Dave Baum's Definitive Guide to Lego Mindstorms*. New York: Springer-Verlag, 2000.

Boxall, John. *Arduino Workshop: A Hands-On Introduction With 65 Projects*. San Francisco, Calif.: No Starch Press, 2013.

Ceceri, Kathy. *Robotics: Discover the Science and Technology of the Future With 20 Projects*. White River Junction, Vt.: Nomad Press, 2012.

Conrad, James M., and Jonathan W. Mills. *Stiquito for Beginners*. Los Alamitos, Calif.: Computer Society, 1999.

Druin, Allison, and James Hendler. *Robots for Kids*. San Francisco, Calif.: Morgan Kaufmann Publishers, 2000.

McComb, Gordon. *The Robot Builder's Bonanza, 4th Edition*. Blue Ridge Summit, Penn.: TAB Books, Inc., 2011.

Sobey, Ed. *Radio-Controlled Car Experiments*. Berkeley Heights, N.J.: Enslow Publishers, Inc. 2011.

——. *Unscrewed: Salvage and Reuse Motors, Gears, Switches, and More From Your Old Electronics*. Chicago: Chicago Review Press, 2011.

——. *Electric Motor Experiments*. Berkeley Heights, N.J.. Enslow Publishers, Inc. 2011.

Valk, Laurens. *The LEGO MINDSTORMS EV3 Discovery Book: A Beginner's Guide to Building and Programming Robots*. San Francisco, Calif.: No Starch Press, 2014.

Magazines

nutsvolts.com

Nuts and Volts. This is a monthly magazine with articles on electronics and technology of interest to robot hobbyists.

robot.com-sub.biz

Robot is a magazine for a broad audience of robot builders.

botmag.com

Robot Magazine is both a helpful Web site and magazine with lots of articles.

servomagazine.com

Servo Magazine is one of the most followed journals for robot builders.

WEB SITES

ipl.org/div/projectguide

The IPL's Science Fair Project Resource Guide will help guide you through your science fair project.

marinetech.org/files/marine/files/Curriculum/Other%20 Curriculum%20Resources/MIROV2MANUAL.pdf

Download this set of instructions to build your own underwater remotely operated vehicle.

robotoid.com

Helpful videos on building robots and more.

sciencebuddies.org/science-fair-projects/project_guide_index. shtml

Let Science Buddies give you extra ideas and tips for your science fair project.

societyofrobots.com

Society of Robots has a helpful section for robot builders and lists of sources for components.

INDEX

A

alternating current (AC), 43
ampere (amp), 51
analog circuits, 105
arms, 108–111
ASIMO, 13

B

batteries
  amp-hours, 78
  benefits, limitations, 34
  care, 77
  dry vs. wet cell, 45
  parallel circuit, 78, 79, 80–81
  principles, 76–78, 81
  rechargeable, 77
  selecting, 76
  series circuit, 77–78, 79, 80–81
  voltage drops, current measurement, 49–53
  voltage measurement, 44–45, 77
boat, motorized
  battery/motor, mounting, 19, 21, 22
  direction, reversing, 23–24
  electric circuit, 18–19, 22, 23–24
  hull, 18, 20
  keel, 23
  motor spin, adjusting, 24–25
  paddles, 26
  propeller, 19–23
  short circuit, 24
  testing, 21–23
  two-motor, 25–27
  voltage, 24–25
  waterline, 19

C

capacitors, 103–104
Capek, Karel, 14
car, motorized
  alligator clip leads, 31–32
  axles, 28–30
  batteries, 34
  body, 28
  electric circuit, 30–32
  motor, 30–32
  propeller, 30–31
  testing, 30, 32
  troubleshooting, 32–34
  wheel drivers, 35, 37
  wheels, 28–30, 35
Chappie, 13
competitions, contests, 112–117
control system
  breadboard, 85, 86
  dedicated slots, 85–86
  EEPROM, 82–83, 91
  power switch, 87
  program, writing, 88
  programmability, 10–13, 82–84
  punch cards, 14–16
  remote control, 84
  servos, connecting, 83, 85–87
  square movement, 99
  STAMP chip, software, 86, 89–93
  straight line movement, 94–97
  turning movement, 97–98
  wiring, 85–88
current measurement, 49–53

D

Devol, George, 16
digital circuits, 105
diodes, 104
direct current (DC), 41–43

E

electricity, fundamental law of, 52
electronics principles, 102–105

F

farads, 104

G

General Motors, 16

H

Hertz, Heinrich, 43
Hollerith, Herman, 14–16

I

IBM, 16
information processing abilities, 12–13
integrated circuits, 105

J

Jacquard, Joseph, 14

Johnny 5, 13

M

mechanical work
  abilities, 10
motors
  disassembly, 41–43
  electricity generation,
    45
  electromagnets, 39–40
  gears, 46–47
  history, 43
  polarity, changing, 40
  principles, 38–40
  selecting, 53, 61
  servo (see servo
    motors)
  speed, 32, 46–47
  stepper, 45–48
  types of, 45–46
  voltage drops, current
    measurement, 49–53
  voltage measurement,
    44–45
  wheels, attachment to,
    64–66
O Ohm's law, 52–53

P

Parallax Web site, 87
platform
  building, 68–71
  circuit board
    attachment, 75
  motor, wheel
    attachment, 72–74
  principles, 67
potentiometers, 55,
  58–59, 87–88, 103

R

remote controlled

devices, 13
resistors, 102–103
robots
  criteria, 10–14
  history, 14–16
  industrial, 10, 14
  tools list, 16–17

S

safety, 9
scientific method, 9
semiconductors, 104–105
sensors
  applications, 12–13,
    100–101, 106
  bump switches,
    100–101, 107
  electronics principles,
    102–105
  infra-red, 106, 108
  light, 100
  photo-resistors, 105,
    107–108
  transducers, 106, 108
servo motors
  controlling (see
    control system)
  described, 45–46, 48,
    53
  drive plate, 58
  hacking method,
    56–59
  hacking principles,
    54–55
  potentiometers, 55,
    58–59, 87–88, 103
  pulse width
    modulation, 92–93
silicon, 104
Sir Plus, 16
South Florida Science

Museum, 16
Stamp II microcontroller,
  85–88

T

torque, 53
transistors, 104

V

Viking 1, Viking 2, 16
voltmeters, 44–53

W

WALL-E, 13
wheels
  arrangement, 62–63
  attachment to motor,
    64–66
  casters, 62
  principles, 61–62
  steering, 62–63
  troubleshooting, 66